Ou... ...s
in Bilingual Education, 1981

Recognized by the National Advisory Council
on Bilingual Education

NATIONAL CLEARINGHOUSE
FOR BILINGUAL EDUCATION

This document is published by InterAmerica Research Associates, Inc., pursuant to contract NIE 400-80-0040 to operate the National Clearinghouse for Bilingual Education. The National Clearinghouse for Bilingual Education is jointly funded by the National Institute of Education and the Office of Bilingual Education and Minority Languages Affairs, U.S. Department of Education. Contractors undertaking such projects under government sponsorship are encouraged to express their judgment freely in professional and technical matters; the views expressed in this publication do not necessarily reflect the views of the sponsoring agencies.

InterAmerica Research Associates, Inc. d/b/a
National Clearinghouse for Bilingual Education
1300 Wilson Boulevard, Suite B2-11
Rosslyn, Virginia 22209
(703) 522-0710/(800) 336-4560

ISBN: 0-89763-067-X
First printing 1982
Printed in USA

10 9 8 7 6 5 4 3 2 1

Contents

Foreword

Outstanding Dissertations in Bilingual Education contains summaries of eleven dissertations recognized by the National Advisory Council on Bilingual Education in 1981. The material presented in this book marks the third year of this competition and represents a growing body of diverse scholarship in the field of bilingual education.

In 1978 Alfredo de los Santos, a member of the National Advisory Council on Bilingual Education, proposed that the council recognize distinguished research in bilingual education by sponsoring an Outstanding Dissertations Competition. De los Santos developed rules and procedures for the competition based on guidelines formulated by other professional organizations such as the International Reading Association, the Council of Community College Professors, and the American Psychological Association. Winners of the 1981 competition were formally announced at the annual meeting of the National Association for Bilingual Education in Boston, Massachusetts, May 23-30, 1981.

One of the activities of the National Clearinghouse for Bilingual Education is to publish documents addressing the specific information needs of the bilingual education community. We are proud to add this distinguished collection of papers to our growing list of publications. Subsequent Clearinghouse publications will similarly seek to contribute information which can assist in the education of minority culture and language groups in the United States.

National Clearinghouse for Bilingual Education

Panel of Judges, 1981
Outstanding Dissertations
National Advisory Council on Bilingual Education

Alfredo G. de los Santos, Jr.,
Chair
Vice Chancellor for Educational
Development
Maricopa Community Colleges
Phoenix, Arizona

Russell N. Campbell, Co-chair
Department of English
University of California at
Los Angeles
Los Angeles, California

Adrian Chan
Office of Research
School of Education
University of Wisconsin
Milwaukee, Wisconsin

Elnora Old Coyote
Director of Fellowship Programs
Montana State University
Bozeman, Montana

Ema T.J. Paviolo
Annville, Pennsylvania

Leonard A. Valverde
Director, Office for Advanced
Research in Hispanic Education
University of Texas at Austin
Austin, Texas

Francis T. Villemain
Dean, School of Education
San Jose State University
San Jose, California

Members of
the National Advisory Council
on Bilingual Education

Astuko Brewer
Laurelhurst School
Seattle, Washington

Russell N. Campbell
Department of English
University of California
   at Los Angeles
Los Angeles, California

Roberto B. Cruz
Director, Berkeley Training
   Resource Center
BABEL, Inc.
Oakland, California

Robert G. Fontenot
Director, Regional Bilingual
   Resource Center
University of Southwestern
   Louisiana
Lafayette, Louisiana

Nilda L. García
Director, Evaluation,
   Dissemination, and Assessment
   Center
Austin, Texas

Richard A. Gresczyk
Indian Education Section
Minneapolis Public Schools
Minneapolis, Minnesota

Seymour Lachman
Baruch College
City University of New York
New York, New York

Carmen Maldonado
Public School 130
Bronx, New York

Ernest J. Mazzone
Massachusetts Department of
   Education
Boston, Massachusetts

María Sánchez
Hartford Board of Education
Hartford, Connecticut

Paul Sandoval
Colorado State Senate
Denver, Colorado

**María Medina-Swanson
   (Seidner)**
Bilingual Education Section
Illinois State Board of Education
Chicago, Illinois

Robert Underwood
Director, Bilingual Training
   Program
University of Guam
Agana, Guam

Francis T. Villemain
Dean, School of Education
San Jose State University
San Jose, California

Gloria Zamora
Inter-Development Research
   Associates
San Antonio, Texas

A Systems Approach to the Development of a Lau Comprehensive Educational Plan: A Theoretical Model for Change

Abelardo Villarreal

First Place, Outstanding Dissertations
National Advisory Council on Bilingual Education

Degree conferred May 1979
The University of Texas
Austin, Texas

Dissertation Committee:
Gloria Contreras, *Chair*
Leonard Valverde
Theodore Andersson
George Blanco
Jo Ann Sweeney

About the Author

Dr. Abelardo Villarreal is associated with the Intercultural Development Research Association (IDRA) as the project director of the Bilingual Education Service Center (BESC) in San Antonio, Texas. He has also served as coordinator of bilingual education programs in the Edgewood and San Antonio school districts in San Antonio. He has taught at the elementary, secondary, and university levels.

SUMMARY

The purpose of this study was to develop and validate a theoretical change model to be used by school districts designing and implementing educational strategies that are compatible with the needs of minority language children (MLC). Emphasis is placed on facilitating the development of a Lau educational plan which focuses on the requirements of the *Lau* v. *Nichols* mandate. The "Lau Remedies" are used as the basis for designing the educational strategies.

The theoretical change model is based on an open systems perspective. As such it identifies the crucial variables affecting the change effort and their interrelationships in an effort to diagnose needs and prescribe educational strategies in a more comprehensive and effective manner. The model should not be considered the panacea for all problems emerging as a result of implementing educational strategies that, frequently, are incongruent with ingrained beliefs and attitudes in a school district. It is designed, however, to alleviate dysfunctional conflict that many times complicates the educational problem addressed in this study.

Three major conclusions were reached. First, the propositional system, after undergoing the test of logical consistency, appeared to provide the basis for empirically evaluating the assumptions that underlie the model. Second, all thirteen propositions were accepted as valid. Three assumptions, however, were found to need some degree of rephrasing. Third, according to the reviewers, the model appeared to be able to perform its intended purpose well. All criteria used to evaluate the utility of the model (simplicity, flexibility, acceptability, and generality) were rated favorably.

STATEMENT OF THE PROBLEM

The most dramatic judicial response to equalizing educational opportunities for minority language children was a Supreme Court decision rendered in 1974. The decision, *Lau* v. *Nichols,* affirmed the authority of the U.S. Department of Health, Education, and Welfare (HEW) to require school districts receiving federal funds to take affirmative action that would assure minority language children of a meaningful education. Furthermore, the decision validated the May 25 Memorandum (issued in 1970 by the U.S. Office for Civil Rights to all school districts) that extended the Civil Rights Act of 1964 to minority language children.

The Office for Civil Rights (OCR) in Washington, D.C. and its ten regional offices were established for the purpose of developing guidelines and monitoring the implementation of the federal mandate, Title VI of the Civil Rights Act of 1964. In order to develop compliance guidelines for districts found in noncompliance with the Lau mandate and the May 25 Memorandum, OCR produced a document known as "Task Force Findings Specifying Remedies Available for Eliminating Past Educational Practices

3

Ruled Unlawful under *Lau* v. *Nichols*." This document is commonly referred to as the "Lau Remedies." Basically, OCR acquires data and information from school districts, analyzes the information, and determines the level of compliance by school districts. The process involves an analysis of the school district's identification and assessment of the children's dominant language, the degree to which the school district provides for participation of minority language children in meaningful educational activities, and the availability and accessibility of adequate instructional staff to deal with the special needs of the minority language children (Littlejohn, 1976).

As of 1975, 334 school districts in the United States were identified for initial compliance review. Of this total, eighty-six were identified in the Dallas regional office. The number of school districts identified for review has not increased, primarily because of limited staff and inadequate funding of the Office for Civil Rights.

School districts found in noncompliance are required to submit a detailed educational plan to OCR (Littlejohn, 1976). Districts may use the "Lau Remedies" as the minimum guidelines or may opt to develop other educational approaches that might better meet the needs of minority language children.

Providing educational approaches to meet the special needs of minority language students will upset the status quo of these school districts, both philosophically and operatively. Rivers (1973) notes that:

> Equalizing educational opportunities for all American children involves a set of conditions and processes that include many more components than normally have been associated with the process of desegregation, . . . that is, [educational approaches must] go beyond the idea that [merely equalizing] physical arrangements. . . is, in fact, equalization of educational opportunities. (p. 11)

Consequently, the development of a plan to meet the educational needs of these children must incorporate the notion that comprehensive change must occur at different levels, if the effort for equal educational opportunity is to have a lasting impact on the children and an emergent philosophical reconceptualization. Research and theory have yet to provide adequate direction to school districts in the process of equalizing educational opportunity.

Bushnell and Rappaport (1971), in their discussion of systems analysis as a viable approach to bringing about change in schools, state:

> What assurance is there that systems analysis offers a more potent change strategy than those examined earlier? The answer lies in the observation that the development of alternative learning strategies through the introduction of new educational technology and the emergence of a unified theory of planned change promises a more effective approach to implementing change. (p. 8)

The experience of school districts when the concept of systems analysis is contemplated appears rather weak and ill defined. Flanagan (1970) attributes this to (1) the lack of assessment techniques to coincide with a precise output system, and (2) the little consideration, if any, given to the significance of the correlation among inputs and the desired and actual outputs of the system.

In order to meet the need for more direction in the development of a detailed educational plan, the study is concerned with conceptualizing a theoretical change model that emphasizes the importance of the analytic and systematic approach to problem identification and problem solving. This model will retain the necessary flexibility to adapt to the unique needs of a school district. Central in this conceptual tool are the following activities: (1) conceptualizing workable solutions; (2) eliciting broad-based community participation (Schreck, 1975); (3) acquiring staff support and commitment at all levels; (4) designing staff development activities to enhance participation in the innovative change; and (5) analyzing the school district's readiness to embark upon a change-related activity.

Mosteller and Moynihan (1972) summarize the problem addressed in the study by stating that:

> What is needed is innovation, experiment, effort, measurement, analysis. What may be hoped for is a process by which the great gaps separating the educational achievement of different ethnic/racial groups begin to narrow. It may be hoped that before the century is out the great gaps will have disappeared. It may also happen that in the process a general theory of education will have evolved, been tested, replicated, and accepted. Just possibly. The creation of this new myth would be a great intellectual achievement, its critique the challenge of the twenty-first century. For the moment, we should strive for equalization. That would be a great social achievement, one the society needs, and one it will probably support with funds, patience, and good sense. (pp. 63-64)

This study proposes to address the problem in relation to an improved and sensitive educational curriculum. Before an attempt is made to address the problem, a set of assumptions must be established relative to the education of MLC and the implementation of educational change.

PURPOSE OF THE STUDY

The purpose of this study is to develop a theoretical model for school districts designing educational strategies to meet the cultural and linguistic needs of minority language children. Two major objectives and a secondary objective guide the study. The first major objective is to review the existing body of knowledge relevant to successful implementation of an innovation and to develop a theoretical change model that school districts can use in designing a meaningful educational plan for MLC. The second major objective is to acquire reactions from change theoreticians and practitioners as to the content validity of the model. The secondary objective is to peruse and synthesize the literature on the conditions for equalizing educational opportunities for minority language children.

DEFINITION OF TERMS

The following definitions indicate how certain terms were used in the study.

- **Change strategy:** A major tactic designed to foster modification to the status quo of the educational system.

- **Comprehensive educational plan:** A set of interrelated activities designed to reach educational goals in a systematic manner. It is used interchangeably with *educational plan, Lau compliance plan,* and *Lau educational plan.*

- **Educational need:** The discrepancy between "what is" and "what should be" in terms of inputs and outputs in the educational system.

- **Educational responses:** A solution that the school district has designed to meet the needs of MLC.

- **Innovation:** Any activity that is new and has implications at all levels in the educational system.

- **Institutional change:** Refers to the modifications made to existing governance structure and educational processes.

- **Lau:** Refers to the requirements inherent in the case, *Lau* v. *Nichols.*

- **Limited English-speaking ability (LESA):** Refers to the student who maintains a less-than-fluent oral language proficiency in English.

- **Minority language child (MLC):** Refers to the child of an identifiable ethnic minority population who maintains some degree of proficiency in a language other than English.

- **Model:** "A representation of a phenomenon which displays the identifiable structural elements of that phenomenon, the relationships among those elements, and the processes involved" (Lippitt, 1973, p. 73).

- **Organizational system:** The sum total of parts working independently or together to achieve educational goals. It is used interchangeably with *educational system.*

- **Proposition:** "Ideas [that] represent outlines of promising hypotheses to improve the process and structure for the educational change" (Frymier, 1969, p. 62).

- **School district:** The smallest legal entity responsible for maintaining an educational system within specific geographic boundaries. It is used interchangeably with *school system* and *public schools.*

METHODOLOGY

Development of the Theoretical Change Model

Chin (1967) defines models as "abstractions from the concreteness of events" (p. 311). Lippitt (1973) describes a model as "... a representation of a phenomenon which displays the identifiable structural elements of that phenomenon, the relationships among those elements, and processes involved" (p. 40). They are conceptual tools that provide the vehicle through which organizations may strengthen their analytic, perceptual, and predictive abilities in an effort to minimize the insecurity and reactionary manifestations that may accompany the introduction of an innovation. Models constitute the blueprints which provide depth and direction to the planning and implementation of innovations.

The basic procedure used to develop the proposed change model evolved after a close and systematic examination of the literature. Emphasis was placed on acquiring information concerning the educational problem being studied, the change process as it relates specifically to the education setting, the comprehensiveness of the proposed solution, and the utility of model building as a tool for facilitating change. The procedure consists of the following five steps:

Step 1: Analysis of the Educational Problem. A clear definition of the problem is necessary before proceeding with decisions on the type and format of a change model. The model builder must establish an objective analysis of the nature and magnitude of the educational problem to be addressed. It is a common principle that the education system should persevere and reach those educational goals that represent realistic expectations of student achievement. Many times this responsibility is truncated, and reactions to existing practices emerge. These reactions or symptoms signal the presence of problems, but fail to pinpoint the factors contributing to the critical situation. A major task of the model builder is to analyze the causal and intervening variables and their effects on the identified symptoms in an effort to define the scope and depth of a particular educational problem. The synthesis of the problem addressed is found in Chapter 4 of the full report of this study.

Step 2: Analysis of the Proposed Solution. The second major task involves the emergence of a solution to the identified problem. In this case it represents the school district's attempt to enhance the equalization of educational opportunities for minority language children. Designing a solution entails the identification of clear and concise goals and objectives, a description of the major change requirements, and an examination of the attributes of the change effort relative to the change process. Zaltman et al. (1977) describe the attributes in the following manner:

- **Relative advantage:** To what degree is the educational solution perceived as serious, realistic, feasible, and advantageous?

- **Impact on social relations:** How are prevalent perceptions and attitudes challenged, and how are existing working relationships modified by the proposed change?

- **Radicalness:** To what degree is the proposed change considered radical and controversial?

- **Compatibility:** How compatible is the proposed change with existing educational practices?

- **Complexity:** How complex is the proposed change, and how familiar is the school district with it?

- **Reversibility:** How easily could the school district return to its original status if the change effort should fail?

- **Divisibility:** Is an experimentation phase an integral part of the proposed change effort?

This analysis provides the plan developer with the framework for describing the content, processes, and relationships necessary to implement the innovation. In other words, it provides the parameters within which the change process can evolve.

Step 3: Delineation of the Theoretical Propositions. For purposes of the study, a propositional system is developed that focuses on the realities of implementing a change effort of this nature and magnitude. A theoretical proposition is defined as a hypothesis that is established relative to the efficient and effective implementation of educational change (Denzin, 1973).

Step 4: Development of a Graphic Representation of the Model. The graphic representation of the change process may facilitate the understanding of the complexities in a change situation, and consequently, improve the ability of the organization to deal with change more effectively and efficiently. The usefulness of the model is enhanced by its ability to show visually the events, interrelationships, and directions of the change effort. Furthermore, success in the graphic representation of the model is an indication of the model builder's ability to analyze, synthesize, and abstract so that the change process becomes more manageable, in this case, for the school district.

Step 5: Description of the Planning and Implementation Processes. Analyzing the complexities of the change process through a model poses a challenge to the model builder. Effective and efficient communication of the message to the client is an important element of a good model. The message must be "loud and clear" and must be exactly as the model builder intended. Lippitt (1973) cautions on the danger of ". . . communication by implication instead of communication by design [as] . . . a reason why so many models are not efficacious" (p. 34). In order to facilitate the comprehension of the model, this study reinforces the graphic representation with an annotation of the procedures involved in the change process.

Validation of the Model

Upon the dissertation committee's recommendation the proposed theoretical model must undergo a validation process. The literature reveals that validation may be acquired from expert judgment, comparisons to other related models, testing in the real world, or simulations and role-playing (Lippitt, 1973). This study focuses on validation through expert judgment as the means to measure the degree to which the theoretical model accomplishes its intended purpose. The process involves a selected number of individuals who possess "expert" knowledge on educational change as it pertains to minority language children. This type of validation is known as *content validity.*

The validation process may be summarized to include the following four activities:

1. Identification of the objectives in the validation process
2. Selection of the persons who will form the panel of experts
3. Determination of the approach to be used in validating the model
4. Development of a reaction form to structure the feedback from the panel of experts.

The validation process of the theoretical model is accomplished through expert judgment. In an effort to minimize the probability of bias when the selection is solely influenced by human choice, this study selects the respondents on the basis of a set of criteria that focuses on the need for a multidisciplinary approach. Furthermore, a predetermined set of criteria tends to standardize the selection process and provide adequate safeguards to maintain a high degree of reliability in the validation process. Principally, the criteria are based on the following factors: knowledge of the change process, experience in the innovative process in education, knowledge of the educational needs of minority language children, and knowledge and experience in organizational development. The selection of the panel of experts requires a careful matching of the individual's qualifications with the aforementioned criteria. In a study involving content validity, it is more important to select the persons best qualified to provide the expert judgment than it is to have a wide sample of respondents.

Development of the Reaction Form. The decision to include a reaction form with the model serves to make sure that the respondents address the objectives set for the validation process and to establish some degree of systematic quantification of responses.

The reaction form is composed of three parts. Part I elicits information relative to the importance of the theoretical propositions. The respondents are asked to rate the importance of the proposition to the proposed change effort and the change process. In addition, the respondent is asked to state a judgment as to the degree to which the model satisfies a particular proposition. Part II addresses the degree to which the model is useful in the implementation of the proposed change. Four criteria are presented in attempting to measure the utility of the model. *Simplicity* refers to the degree to which the theoretical model is realistic, manageable, and readable. *Flexibility* refers to the degree to which the theoretical model allows for adjustments and modifications. *Applicability* addresses the degree to which the model depicts a synthesis of reality and is appropriate for the educational setting. *Generality* refers to the degree to which the model is applicable to varying sizes of school districts, differing educational philosophies, and other differing basic characteristics. The respondents are asked to make a judgment as to the model's utility by assigning a rating in each criterion. Then the respondents are asked to elaborate on that judgment.

Part III requests additional information that the respondents may have relative to the utility of the model. The respondents possess a wealth of information that surpasses whatever the form may be able to elicit.

THE PARADIGM

Basic Theoretical Propositions

Knezevich (1975) suggests that attempting to address all factors in a model may create a model that is incomprehensible and complex, therefore reducing its usefulness and viability. He alludes to a model as a "symbolic approximation of a real situation" and, as such, it may be intentionally incomplete. The task of the model builder includes the selection of those pertinent factors that may affect significantly the implementation of a change effort. These factors are incorporated into "ideas [that] represent outlines of promising hypotheses to improve the process and structure for the educational change" (Frymier, 1969, p. 62).

There are two major limitations that must be considered in using the model. First, it is based on assumptions that are peculiar to an educational situation that is surrounded by strong emotional factors. Thus, overgeneralizing its usefulness with different educational situations may prove dangerous. Second, the model builder could have inadvertently infused personal opinions through his interpretations of available data. Murphy (1977) states that "... the process of applying models has forced us to become aware that there is no such thing as a neutral, unbiased observer" (p. 569).

The dissertation includes a discussion of the major variable clusters in the educational environment. The following propositions evolve from this discussion:

Change Stimulus

1. The greater the real or imagined threat to the organization's status quo, the greater the resistance to play the traditional role of responding in time of national crisis.

2. The greater the external pressure experienced in a school district to improve student achievement, the higher the likelihood that it will consider some form of change.

3. The greater the internal pressure to improve student achievement, the greater the chances to undertake successful alternative instructional strategies that may deviate from existing practices.

4. The more the stimulus subsides, the greater the difficulties in maintaining sufficient commitment to promote the implementation and formal adoption of alternative instructional strategies.

Scope of the Change

5. The more the organization perceives the alternate instructional strategies as beneficial and compatible with existing practices, the more likely it is to accept the change.

6. The more the goals of the change effort are achieved in the implementation phase, the greater the likelihood that the school district will maintain and institutionalize the alternative instructional strategies.

Institutional Setting

7. The less management perceives the change effort as threatening its management prerogatives, the higher the chances to increase its commitment to the continuation of the alternative instructional strategies.

8. The greater the perceived administrative and collegial support at all levels toward the alternative instructional strategies, the greater the opportunity for these strategies' successful implementation and formal adoption.

9. Commitment to embark on specific change efforts will develop when groups and individuals within the school organization do not attempt to block the efforts to implement alternative instructional strategies.

10. The greater the perceived synchronization of the new role requirements with the normal daily routine, the greater the chances for facilitating the implementation and formal adoption of alternative instructional strategies.

11. The greater the planning team represents a microcosm of the entire organization, the less the chances for the plan to reflect fragmentary and narrow spheres of interest.

12. The more individuals are involved in the planning and encouraged to participate in the decisionmaking process, the higher the likelihood that they will accept and support the change effort.

13. The greater the individual security with the change effort, the greater the chances to experiment and formally adopt new ideas.

MODEL DESCRIPTION

The proposed model is characterized by the following: (1) a systematic approach; (2) an emphasis on the importance of products as well as the processes through which the products were obtained; (3) the incorporation of strategies to build a school district's capabilities in the areas of planning, diagnosing, and decisionmaking; (4) a provision for broad input and validation of needs and activities from parents, teachers, students, and administrators; (5) a comprehensive needs assessment; (6) alternative methods to organizing and mobilizing school personnel for plan design and implementation; and (7) a management system. The description is divided into two sections: the involvement stages and the phases.

Involvement Stages

A major assumption underlying the theoretical model is that thinking and feeling are closely linked in that thinking is influenced by feelings, and feelings are not devoid of content. The implication is that the model must comprehensively address the change effort in conjunction with the existing psychological climate in the school district. Psychological factors pose major barriers to a change effort that is surrounded by hostility, fears, and prejudices (Pizer and Travers, 1975). This is the case with equalizing educational opportunities for minority language students.

An important prerequisite to the implementation of this change effort is the establishment of a psychological climate that promotes objectivity and deflects irrationality in decisionmaking. Experience in the field reveals that school districts developing a Lau educational plan often fail to show the positive disposition and psychological climate conducive to the participatory planning activities proposed in the model. Participatory planning entails the cooperation of individuals and the coordination of the best thinking toward a common purpose. Invariably, school district personnel begin the innovative process by asking inappropriate questions, making invalid assumptions, and attempting to manipulate the wrong variables. Consequently, the recalcitrant school district finds itself arriving at an irrational consensus.

Psychological maturity represents a major goal of the change effort. It is referred to as the state of mind that is characterized by independent thinking, a feeling of closeness, unity of purpose, and mature approach to controversy. It represents a state where the organization promotes change and pushes toward the successful realization of its equal educational opportunity objectives.

For purposes of the study, five involvement stages reflecting distinct dimensions of the psychological climate are identified. Each dimension reflects a behavioral pattern that parallels the school district's readiness for equal educational opportunity. It is consistent with the impact that change events have on the organization. These dimensions are characterized by periods of time when certain change-related activities may be better received and more productive. The time span of each stage is strongly related to the readiness and willingness of the school district to embark on the particular change effort.

Within each involvement stage, specific activities related to the different phases in the change process are considered. These activities are distinct in that they represent certain decisions that are consistent with the behavioral pattern characteristics of a particular involvement stage.

The five involvement stages are described in the dissertation proper. The discussion includes the implications that each particular stage has on the change process, the affective objectives that the change effort must address, and the transition clues that serve as guideposts in determining a change in the involvement status.

Phases in the Change Effort

The change effort is analytically divided into six major phases which, in practice, constitute the critical path (e.g., activities, processes) of the innovative process. The activities and processes within each phase are conditioned by the involvement stages of the school district. It must be noted that the chronological flow of activities in each phase is interrupted to address concurrent activities in the other phases that complement the particular involvement stage. In other words, a completed phase is not necessarily a prerequisite to beginning the next phase. The proper timing of the activity in relation to the involvement stage is central to the successful planning and implementation of the change effort.

The dissertation includes a description of each of the following phases:
  I: Sensing a Need
 II: Mobilizing to Plan a Response
III: Planning the Response
IV: Mobilizing to Implement the Response
 V: Implementing the Response
VI: Incorporating a Response

CONCLUSIONS

The conclusions of this study fall into categories that correspond to the objectives set for the validation process. They are discussed in this section in the following manner:

1. Conclusions regarding the relevance of the propositional system and the degree to which the model satisfies the propositions

2. Conclusions regarding the utility of the model in light of the Office for Civil Rights' requirements for an educational compliance plan that aims at enhancing equal educational opportunities for minority language children.

At a minimum, changes will be recommended any time at least two of the reviewers agree that certain modifications will strengthen the power of the model.

Upon analyzing the data obtained on the relevance of the propositional system, a number of conclusions were reached pertaining to the addition, deletion, and modification of the propositions. First, it appears that the propositional system provides the basis for empirically evaluating the assumptions that underlie the theoretical model. Second, the data reveal that clarification and refocusing of some propositions will strengthen the power of the model significantly. Specifically, the following conclusions were reached:

1. The propositional system plays a very important role in understanding the model. It provides the foundation upon which the model is built.

2. The thirteen propositions appear to be valid. In some instances, suggestions were made for rephrasing or refocusing certain propositions.

3. The comments reveal that propositions underwent the test of logical consistency, which is one of the three tests that Denzin (1973) suggests are crucial in attempting to evaluate a propositional system. Overall, this suggested propositional system appears to offer the logical consistency required.

4. A decision was made to include only those propositions with a mean rating of 5.0 or above. Five is the midpoint in the scale. All the propositions whose mean rating was 7.0 or above were categorized as "essential"; those whose mean rating was between and including 5.5 and 6.9 were categorized as "very important"; and those whose mean ratings were between and including 5.0 and 5.4 were labeled "somewhat important." Using the aforementioned criteria, eight propositions qualified as *essential*, four as *very important*, and one as *somewhat important*.

The model responds to a serious concern in the change literature regarding "dignify[ing] change by reason of faith, good intentions, and administrative fiat as constituting a theory of change" (Sarason, 1971, p. 19). From the analysis of the ratings and comments it may be interpreted that the model possesses potential in performing its intended purpose well. First, the model offers simplicity, a characteristic that is consistently lacking in many educational change models. Second, its flexibility to allow for adjustments and modifications becomes an important attribute of the model. This is crucial at a time when current implementation literature is reflecting the need for eclectic implementation approaches that consider the institutional setting as well as the requirements of the innovative effort in planning effective and efficient implementation techniques (Berman, 1979).

Third, applicability proved to be, according to the rating obtained, an attribute of the model. It can be said that the model provides a blueprint that approximates reality and is a good "representation of a phenomenon which displays the identifiable structural elements of that phenomenon, the relationships among those elements and processes involved" (Lippitt, 1973, p. 40).

Last, the model can be used by a school district of any size. The process orientation of the model allows for the basic elements that must be present in any change effort. Nevertheless, the extent of the implementation activities will be determined by a number of other variables.

REFERENCES

Berman, P. "Designing Implementation to Match Policy Situation: A Contingency Analysis of Programmed and Adaptive Implementation." Unpublished manuscript, 1979.

Best, J.W. *Research in Education.* 2d ed. Englewood Cliffs, N.J.: Prentice-Hall, 1970.

Bushnell, D.S., and Rappaport, C. *Planned Change in Education: A Systems Approach.* New York: Harcourt, Brace Jovanovich, 1971.

Chin, R. "Some Ideas on Changing." In *Perspective on Educational Change.* New York: Appleton-Century Crofts, 1967.

Denzin, N.K. *The Research Act: A Theoretical Introduction to Sociological Methods.* Chicago: Aldine Publishing Co., 1973.

Flanagan, J. "How Instructional Systems Will Manage Learning." *Nation's Schools* 86 (October 1970): 68.

Frymier, J.R. *Fostering Educational Change.* Columbus, Ohio: Charles E. Merrill Publishing Co., 1969.

Gay, L.R. *Educational Research: Competencies for Analysis and Application.* Columbus, Ohio: Charles E. Merrill Publishing Co., 1976.

Knezevich, S.J. *Administration of Public Education.* New York: Harper & Row, 1975.

Lau v. *Nichols,* 414 U.S. 563 (1974).

Likert, R. *The Human Organization: Its Management and Value.* New York: McGraw-Hill, 1967.

Lippitt, G.L. *Visualizing Change: Model Building and the Change Process.* La Jolla, Calif.: University Associates, 1973.

Littlejohn, J. "The Lau Issue." Paper presented at the Ten Regional Interstate Planning Project, 19 November 1976, San Antonio, Tex.

Moser, C.A. *Survey Methods in Social Investigation.* London: Heinemann, 1966.

Mostellar, F., and Moynihan, D.P. "A Pathbreaking Report." In *Equality of Educational Opportunity.* New York: Vintage Books, 1972.

Murphy, J.T. "Musings on the Utility of Decision-Making Models." *Harvard Educational Review* 47 (November 1977): 565-569.

Pizer, S., and Travers, J.R. *Psychology and Social Change.* New York: McGraw-Hill, 1975.

Rivers, C. "The Development of a Planning Guide for Comprehensive Change through the Process of Desegregation." Ph.D. dissertation, Ohio State University, 1973.

Sarason, S.B. *The Culture of the School and the Problem of Change.* Boston: Allyn and Bacon, 1971.

U.S., Civil Rights Act of 1964. P.L. 88-352.

Zaltman, G.; Florio, D.H.; and Sikorski, L.A. *Dynamic Educational Change.* New York: The Free Press, 1977.

(These references are part of the list of over 200 references used in the dissertation.)

Miscue Corrections by Bilingual and Monolingual Teachers When Teaching Bilingual Children to Read:
A Comparative Survey in Wales, Spain, and Regions of the United States

Jesús Cortéz

Second Place, Outstanding Dissertations
National Advisory Council on Bilingual Education

Degree conferred May 1980
University of Washington
Seattle, Washington

Dissertation Committee:
Sam Sebesta, *Chair*
Dianne L. Monson
James Vásquez
Carol Gray
James Banks
Claudia Arenas

About the Author

Dr. Jesús Cortéz is assistant professor and coordinator for bilingual education at the California State University at Chico School of Education. He has
been field coordinator of the University of Washington's Bilingual Graduate
Fellowship Program and a national bilingual fellow at the same institution.

SUMMARY

Who should teach bilingual children to read? What type of instruction is likely to relate bilingualism to reading behavior in a positive way? These questions are addressed through data obtained from cross-cultural, international sources.

The basic question is whether bilingual and monolingual teachers differ in the way they correct the oral reading of bilingual children. The type and number of corrections a teacher makes while a child reads orally (whether or not textual meaning is intact) provides evidence for that teacher's philosophical orientation toward reading instruction and may also relate to the degree of the teacher's preparation, the teacher's regional background, or the teacher's language background.

The subjects were 144 teachers—18 monolingual and 18 bilingual teachers from each of four regions: Wales, Spain, and two regions of the United States (Southwest and Northwest). Findings revealed that bilingual teachers, compared with monolingual teachers, tended to correct oral reading deviations that interfere with the meaning of the text more than they corrected those deviations that do not interfere with the meaning.

Implications are that bilingual teachers appear to follow the meaning-centered reading instruction model more frequently than monolingual teachers do, which may result in better reading comprehension. Bilingual teacher superiority identified in this study is not consistent across all regions and needs to be examined further by region.

STATEMENT OF THE PROBLEM

This study grew out of a concern to provide needed research into the field of bilingual education and reading. It was based on the experimenter's belief in the benefits of bilingualism, bilingual education, and, in particular, the application of bilingualism in the area of reading comprehension. Specifically, the study attempted to explore the following: When reading teachers correct bilingual children's reading miscues, what might occur if (1) the teacher is bilingual in the same two languages as the bilingual student; (2) the teacher is monolingual and does not speak the child's native language; (3) the teacher is bilingual and highly prepared in reading; (4) the teacher is monolingual and highly prepared in reading; (5) the teacher is bilingual and less prepared in reading; (6) the teacher is from Wales, Spain, or the United States; (7) the teacher approaches correction with either a meaning or code emphasis?

The experimenter developed a system of classification of meaning and non-meaning change miscues, based on Kenneth Goodman's theory of reading instruction (Goodman, 1965a; Goodman, 1965b; and Goodman and Burke, 1972). For purposes of this study, the meaning change category was divided into three subheadings: syntactic meaning change, graphonic meaning change, and interference meaning change. When classified under these subheadings, the reader's miscue changes the meaning of the text. The non-meaning change category was divided into three subheadings: syntactic non-meaning change, graphonic non-meaning change, and interlanguage non-meaning change. When classified under these subheadings, the reader's miscues do not change meaning in the text or disrupt the author's intended meaning, and comprehension of the author's message and the reader's response are matched.

PURPOSE OF THE STUDY

There has always been controversy over which methods of reading instruction are most effective in teaching children to read. This issue has become one of greater importance with the inclusion of bilingual methodology in the institutionalized curriculum of reading. The responsibility of teaching reading to a heterogeneous population must be one of primary concern to reading educators, especially when some of the students are learning to read a second language.

In an attempt to fulfill this task, this study develops a theoretical position of reading instruction and explores this position as it contrasts the performance of monolingual and bilingual teachers. Indirectly the study provides insights that may account for some bilingual children's lower-than-grade-level performance in reading achievement, as evidenced by their lower standardized test scores and their tendency to drop out of school earlier than their monolingual peers (Carter, 1970; Carter and Segura, 1979). It provides research that synthesizes philosophy and implements philosophy in classroom practice. This is necessary if educators are to face the task of promoting quality education for all ethnically, racially, culturally, or linguistically different children.

DEFINITION OF TERMS

- **Miscues:** Oral reading deviations from text. "The phenomenon that occurs when a reader deviates from the expected response" (Sims, 1979; Goodman and Burke, 1972).

- **Meaning change miscue:** A miscue that is not consistent with the meaning of the text (e.g., "The boy is *hoarse / house*").

- **Non-meaning change miscue:** A miscue that does not alter the meaning of the text (e.g., "The boy is walking in the *forest / woods*").

- **Syntactic miscue:** (1) Meaning change—the grammatical function does result in change of meaning of the text (e.g., "He did not realize what could happen to him because *of the new law / he was new and old*"). (2) Non-meaning change—the grammatical function does not result in a change of meaning of the text (e.g., "One day in the early 1800s a *black man / man black* was born in America").

- **Graphonic miscue:** (1) Meaning change—some degree of graphic and sound similarity exists but the miscue does result in change of meaning of the text (e.g., "They belonged to White / *wheat* masters"). (2) Non-meaning change—some degree of graphic and sound similarity exists but the miscue does not result in change of meaning of the text (e.g., "White masters ruled their lives from the *moment / minute* they were born until they finally died").

- **Interlanguage non-meaning change miscues:** "An interlanguage incorporates characteristics of both the native and the target language of the learner" (Hakuta and Cancino, 1977, p. 297). Miscues originating in the child's first language that do not change meaning (e.g., "He desperately tried to *escape / escaparse*").

- **Interference meaning change miscues:** Miscues whose source can be traced back to the learner's native language (Hakuta and Cancino, 1977, p. 297) with the added proviso that they interfere with meaning (e.g., "The law meant that a black who had been born free could suddenly be turned into a slave if he entered certain states where slavery was *permitted / primitivo*").

- **High prepared:** Teachers with relatively greater formal preparation in reading pedagogy.

- **Low prepared:** Teachers with relatively less formal preparation in reading pedagogy.

- **Monolingual:** Teachers who cannot read or comprehend the first language of the child. Identification based on supervisor and teacher self-evaluation.

- **Bilingual:** Teachers who can read and comprehend the first language of the child. Identification based on supervisor and teacher self-evaluation.

- **Synthetic:** Instructional and philosophical orientation emphasizing decoding as crucial toward learning to read.

- **Analytic:** Instructional and philosophical orientation emphasizing comprehension and meaning as crucial toward learning to read.

SAMPLING

The investigator prepared three transcripts: Welsh-English, Catalán-Castellaño, and Spanish-English. These were used, respectively, in Wales, Spain, and the United States regions. Each transcript contained fifty-four miscues divided equally between two categories: those that interfered with meaning and those that did not. The miscues were further subcategorized according to linguistic levels: syntactic, graphonic, and interlanguage/interference.

The subjects were 144 teachers: 18 monolingual and 18 bilingual teachers from each of the four regions. Each was asked to indicate which of the miscues he or she would correct in a child's oral reading. According to each sample by region, an original repeated measures design instrument was administered with the dependent variable being the mean number of miscues a teacher reported that he or she would correct. Bilingual and monolingual responses were moderated by teacher preparation (high and low) and teacher-reported philosophy (analytic and synthetic). A one-way analysis of variance, with $p < 0.05$, was calculated for each of the five research questions by country and summarized by total for all countries.

THEORETICAL FOUNDATIONS

The theoretical foundation of this dissertation is based on a trio of contrasting theories, which are briefly outlined in this section. First, there are two views of teaching reading: the analytic view, which is meaning centered, holistic, and child oriented, and the synthetic, which focuses on automatic responses, identification of letters, patterns, and correction of deviations from text. Second, two contrasting views of second language acquisition are reviewed: the interlanguage view, which holds that the second language builds on the first and has characteristics of both, and the interference view, which maintains that the first language impedes second language learning. Third, and drawing heavily upon the above theories of reading instruction and second language acquisition, are two contrasting views of instruction, which in practice reveal a teacher's philosophy about bilingual children. The difference model views children's cultural and linguistic differences as assets; the deficit model identifies children's cultural and linguistic differences as weaknesses that must be eradicated.

Bilingualism and Reading

Reading instruction is challenged by a controversy concerning bilingualism, a dynamic controversy that demands that knowledge about second language acquisition be applied to reading instruction. Specifically, it involves the implementation of reading strategies through the medium of not only the target language, but also the child's native language.

Educators have become aware of the comparatively lower reading performance of bilingual children (Vásquez, 1978; Carter, 1970; Carter and Segura, 1979; García, 1974; Feitelson, 1976). Since literacy is one of the most essential abilities, teachers need to accept responsibility for aiding bilingual children to attain reading skills.

Buck (1973), in discussing the miscues of nonnative speakers of English, maintains that the reading process is essentially the same across languages; it is the strategies and instruction that may vary, and that ultimately affect the learner. However, unique provisions for teaching reading to bilinguals must be considered. For example, the reading proficiency for bilingual children might be enhanced if reading instruction is initiated in their native language (Osterberg, 1961; Modiano, 1968).

Theory in the field of reading is often contradictory. The Goodman model, classified as the *analytic method*, and the model represented by the *synthetic method* offer opposing views. The question becomes one not just of sequencing but also of emphasis in the analytic versus the synthetic modes of instruction. Where the sequence and emphasis in the analytic mode would proceed in beginning reading instruction from syntax and progress to morphology and then to phonology, the synthetic mode would base instruction in reading in the reverse order: first with phonology, then morphology, and finally syntax.

The analytic view maintains that readers first need to comprehend the material they are reading whether or not their responses deviate from the exact written text. Proponents of this view argue that the synthetic model entails misguided drill, the material the children must read is dull, and the result of teaching reading with this model is to develop word callers, not readers (K. Goodman, 1975; Groff, 1978).

The synthetic view holds that teaching must be systematic and requires exact correlation between what the text says and what the readers read. According to the synthetic model, by far the best way to achieve this is to develop a strong decoder (Jeffrey and Samuels, 1967; Walcutt, Lamport, and McCracken, 1974). Proponents of this model argue that the analytic model encourages guessing and is unsystematic because it has no vocabulary control.

It is clear that, although each group agrees that the final objective in teaching reading is to develop proficient readers, there is disagreement on the philosophies and methods by which to attain that end.

REVIEW OF RESEARCH AND THEORY ON SECOND LANGUAGE ACQUISITION

Theories of Second Language Acquisition

Understanding how language is acquired and learned in the first and second language environments is crucial to the teaching of reading. This is especially true since the establishment and institutionalization of bilingual education in the reading classroom. Central to comprehending the situation is an understanding of the two differing views of second language acquisition research: the interference view and the interlanguage view.

When two languages vary in the learner's system at the graphonic, syntactic, and semantic levels, the teacher has an option on how best to evaluate the learner's deviations. This evaluation in many cases will be based on the teacher's view of second language acquisition. The deviation, for instance, may be considered an error or an assumed deficit in the learner's use of language (Bereiter and Engelman, 1966). A differing view is that the deviation is natural and representative of the learner's deeper linguistic construct (Selinker, 1972).

The interference view of second language acquisition may be considered a deficit model because the learner is not consistently accurate when using language as evaluated against an accepted norm or standard, usually in the target language. Teachers who correct these deviations at the graphic and syntactic levels most likely do so because they may assume that the interference that occurs between languages, if not corrected, will eventually result in delayed learning for the bilingual child.

However, the alternative interlanguage view of second language acquisition would result in teachers' approaching evaluation differently. Because it is psycholinguistic in nature, interlanguage is considered a structured language system. Therefore, when interlanguage occurs, it is considered the learners' attempts to bring meaning to their speech. "The utterances of such a learner are not mistakes or deviant forms, but rather are part of a separate but nevertheless a genuine linguistic system" (Schumann, 1974, p. 145). Teachers who hold this interlanguage view would therefore evaluate bilingual learners' deviations based on meaning as manifestations of growth in language skill in bilingual children. Teacher evaluation would be based on whether the speaker expresses meaning at all levels: graphonic, syntactic, and semantic. While proponents of the interference view would then evaluate all deviations as "errors," the proponents of the interlanguage view would be more likely to evaluate them in terms of the learners' attempts to express meaning.

MAIN HYPOTHESIS

The study examined the following main research question: **Is there a difference in the types of reading miscues bilingual and monolingual reading teachers correct in the reading of bilingual children?**

In order to examine the main question fully, the following questions were asked:

1. **Do highly prepared bilinguals correct differently than highly prepared monolinguals?**

2. **Do analytic bilinguals correct differently than analytic monolinguals?**

3. **Do synthetic bilinguals correct differently than synthetic monolinguals?**

The questions were transformed into research questions which tested three hypotheses. The following example presents the transformation of research question one into hypotheses which place direction or projected findings in categories of reading miscues:

Example: Will bilingual teachers by country and by total of all countries be more sensitive than monolingual teachers in terms of correcting meaning change miscues? This question is tested by the following three hypotheses:

1. Bilingual teachers, compared with monolingual teachers, will correct fewer non-meaning change miscues (subcategories syntactic, graphonic, and interlanguage).

2. Bilingual teachers, compared with monolingual teachers, will correct more meaning change miscues (subcategories syntactic, graphonic, and interference).

3. The difference between meaning change corrections and non-meaning change corrections (subcategories syntactic, graphonic, and interlanguage/interference) will be greater for bilingual than for monolingual teachers.

FINDINGS AND CONCLUSIONS

Findings indicate a trend favoring bilingual teachers, compared with monolingual teachers, in terms of the Goodman theory of miscue correction. Out of the possible 300 comparisons pertinent to the five stated questions, fifty-two were significant. Of the fifty-two significant findings, forty-five supported the hypothesis that bilingual teachers corrected meaning and did not correct non-meaning miscues, compared with their monolingual counterparts; seven of the findings indicated stronger Goodman theory performance by monolinguals. Hence it may be concluded that these findings favor the bilingual teachers as supporting the model.

With regard to region, however, these findings are not upheld in the Northwest United States. In fact, all seven significant findings favoring monolingual support of the Goodman model were drawn from the Northwest United States sample. Findings indicate that there were no significant differences between the corrections made by low-prepared bilinguals and low-prepared monolinguals in Wales, Spain, and the Southwest United States. Again, in the Northwest United States the findings indicate that monolingual low-prepared teachers supported the Goodman model at all three levels. Comparisons by type of preparation, analytic to synthetic, indicated that analytically trained bilinguals favored the Goodman model in Spain and the Southwest United States, with no significant differences in Wales. It may be concluded that findings are generally supportive of the use of bilingual teachers to teach reading to bilingual children provided that research supports the model on which the study is based. (For a further analysis of research questions one through five refer to the summary of analysis of variance tables in the Appendix.)

IMPLICATIONS

The most consistent finding with regard to this sample, if one accepts the Goodman model of reading, is that bilingual teachers are better able to work with bilingual children, than monolingual teachers. This is based on the finding that bilingual teachers correct meaning change, while accepting without correction the miscues that do not change meaning. This pattern's near-consistency across countries, regions, and language indicates support for the bilingual teacher's emphasis on meaning. If this emphasis is utmost in the pattern of bilingual teachers, it is a strong argument in support of using bilingual teachers to teach reading to bilingual children because they are better able to support meaning orientation when deviations are influenced by the children's native language.

The findings in the Northwest United States are inconsistent with the other regions. If a district's policy consistently adopts the Goodman philosophy as its orientation, then serious consideration must be given to why bilingual teachers in the Northwest did not support the Goodman model. Further, training policies for teacher preparation programs must also be evaluated to see if this is an area that may explain an orientation consistent with the responses bilingual teachers made. Consistent with this policy may be the ever-present awareness of the shortage of trained bilingual teachers and staff. The hiring of nonprofessional teachers may be productive only if their hiring is adequately reinforced with special activities such as workshops that will train teachers in consistent, productive theory of miscue analysis and correction.

Major emphasis on correction was on the interlanguage/interference level, indicating that knowledge of the first language is necessary in order to be consistent with the Goodman theory when dealing with reading instruction in a second language. It was an advantage for bilingual teachers to know that the miscue was either interference (one that changed meaning) or interlanguage (one that did not change the meaning of the text).

The next most frequent significant difference was at the graphonic level. Where monolingual teachers may believe that children's mispronunciation of a particular word is important, the bilingual teachers' view is that in some instances meaning remains despite mispronunciation. The teaching methodology that aims at improving the self-concept of bilingual children is often patterned drill, on a literal level of comprehension, and with a strong emphasis on pronunciation. This approach to language and reading is not natural communication. What is more, it often forces bilingual children to become self-conscious of sounds they may not be able to make or hear, and reinforces the children's weaknesses. The ultimate effect on bilingual children is likely to be negative; lowered self-concept results because children search for meaning in what they do. Hence, such an approach is unproductive in enhancing children's reading skills.

If one is to follow the Goodman philosophy, then teachers must be trained to see that synthetic training based on patterned drill and overcorrection of non-meaning change miscues is often self-defeating in developing meaning-based reading. Patterned, literal, and dull language exercises will fail to elicit language production or interest in bilingual children. Rather, a teacher's orientation to meaning-based instruction with an analytic teaching philosophy in reading would be likely to build on a bilingual child's strengths. This point of view would indicate that constant repetition should no longer be used as a method to eradicate differences in pronunciation; rather, the goal would focus on the message, the meaning.

APPENDIX

Table 5

**Research Question One: Summary of ANOVA Results
Comparing Monolingual and Bilingual Teachers**

Country/ Category	IA Non-Meaning Change	IB Meaning Change	IC Meaning minus Non-Meaning Change
Wales			
Syntactic	–	–	–
Graphonic	–	–	–
Interl/f	–	M< B*	–
Total	–	–	–
Spain			
Syntactic	–	–	–
Graphonic	M >B*	M<B*	M<B*
Interl/f	–	M<B*	M<B*
Total	–	M<B*	M<B*
Southwest			
Syntactic	–	–	–
Graphonic	–	–	–
Interl/f	–	M<B*	–
Total	–	M<B*	–
Northwest			
Syntactic	–	M >B*	–
Graphonic	–	–	–
Interl/f	M >B*	–	–
Total	–	M >B*	–
All Countries			
Syntactic	–	–	–
Graphonic	M >B*	–	M<B*
Interl/f	–	M<B*	M<B*
Total	–	–	M<B*

*Significant at $p \leq .05$

Table 11

Research Question Two: Summary of ANOVA Results Comparing High-Prepared Monolingual and Bilingual Teachers

Country/ Category	IIA Non-Meaning Change	IIB Meaning Change	IIC Meaning minus Non-Meaning Change
Wales			
Syntactic	–	–	–
Graphonic	–	–	–
Interl/f	–	M<B*	–
Total	–	–	–
Spain			
Syntactic	–	–	–
Graphonic	M>B*	M<B*	M<B*
Interl/f	–	M<B*	M<B*
Total	–	M<B*	M<B*
Southwest			
Syntactic	–	M<B*	–
Graphonic	–	–	–
Interl/f	–	–	–
Total	–	M<B*	–
Northwest			
Syntactic	–	–	–
Graphonic	–	–	–
Interl/f	–	–	–
Total	–	–	–
All Countries			
Syntactic	–	–	–
Graphonic	–	–	–
Interl/f	–	M<B*	M<B*
Total	–	–	–

*Significant at $p \leq .05$

Table 17

Research Question Three: Summary of ANOVA Results Comparing Low-Prepared Monolingual and Bilingual Teachers

Country/ Category	IIIA Non-Meaning Change	IIIB Meaning Change	IIIC Meaning minus Non-Meaning Change
Wales			
Syntactic	–	–	–
Graphonic	–	–	–
Interl/f	–	–	–
Total	–	–	–
Spain			
Syntactic	–	–	–
Graphonic	–	–	–
Interl/f	–	–	–
Total	–	–	–
Southwest			
Syntactic	–	–	–
Graphonic	–	–	–
Interl/f	–	–	–
Total	–	–	–
Northwest			
Syntactic	–	M >B*	–
Graphonic	–	M >B*	–
Interl/f	–	M >B*	–
Total	–	M >B*	–
All Countries			
Syntactic	–	–	–
Graphonic	–	–	–
Interl/f	–	–	M<B*
Total	–	–	–

*Significant at $p \leq .05$

Table 23

Research Question Four: Summary of ANOVA Results Comparing Analytic Monolingual and Bilingual Teachers

Country/ Category	IVA Non-Meaning Change	IVB Meaning Change	IVC Meaning minus Non-Meaning Change
Wales			
Syntactic	–	–	–
Graphonic	–	–	–
Interl/f	–	–	–
Total	–	–	–
Spain			
Syntactic	–	–	–
Graphonic	M>B*	–	M<B*
Interl/f	–	–	M<B*
Total	–	–	–
Southwest			
Syntactic	–	M<B*	–
Graphonic	–	–	–
Interl/f	–	–	–
Total	–	–	M<B*
Northwest			
Syntactic	–	M>B*	–
Graphonic	–	–	–
Interl/f	–	–	–
Total	–	–	–
All Countries			
Syntactic	–	–	–
Graphonic	–	–	–
Interl/f	–	–	M<B*
Total	–	–	–

*Significant at p ≤ .05

Table 29

**Research Question Five: Summary of ANOVA Results Comparing
Synthetic Monolingual and Bilingual Teachers**

Country/ Category	VA Non-Meaning Change	VB Meaning Change	VC Meaning minus Non-Meaning Change
Wales			
Syntactic	–	–	–
Graphonic	–	–	–
Interl/f	–	M< B*	–
Total	–	–	–
Spain			
Syntactic	–	–	–
Graphonic	–	–	M< B*
Interl/f	–	M< B*	–
Total	–	M< B*	–
Southwest			
Syntactic	–	–	–
Graphonic	–	–	–
Interl/f	–	M< B*	–
Total	–	–	–
Northwest			
Syntactic	–	–	–
Graphonic	–	–	–
Interl/f	–	–	–
Total	–	–	–
All Countries			
Syntactic	–	–	–
Graphonic	M >B*	–	M< B*
Interl/f	–	M< B*	M< B*
Total	–	–	M< B*

*Significant at $p \leq .05$

REFERENCES

Bereiter, C., and Engelmann, S. *Teaching Disadvantaged Children in the Preschool.* Englewood Cliffs, N.J.: Prentice-Hall, 1966.

Bucker, Catherine. "Miscues of Non-Native Speakers of English." In *Miscue Analysis,* edited by K. Goodman. Urbana, Ill.: National Council of Teachers of English, 1973.

Carter, Thomas. *Mexican Americans in Schools: A History of Educational Neglect.* New York: College Entrance Examination Board, 1970.

_____, and Segura, Roberto D. *Mexican Americans in School—A Decade of Change.* New York: College Entrance Examination Board, 1979.

Feitelson, Dina, ed. *Mother Tongue or Second Language, On the Teaching of Reading in Multilingual Societies.* Sixth Annual IRA Congress on Reading. Newark, Del.: International Reading Association, 1976.

García, R. "Mexican American Bilingualism and English Language Development." *Journal of Reading* 7, no. 6 (March 1974): 467-73.

Goodman, Kenneth. "Dialect Barriers to Reading Comprehension." *Elementary English* 42 (1965a): 639-43.

_____ . "A Linguistic Study of Cues and Miscues in Reading." *Elementary Education* 42 (1965b): 853-60.

_____ . "Do You Have to Be Smart to Read: Do You Have to Read to Be Smart?" *Reading Teacher* 28, no. 7 (1975): 625-32.

Goodman, Yetta, and Burke, Carolyn. *Reading Miscue Inventory.* New York: Macmillan, 1972.

Groff, Patrick. "Should Children Learn to Read Words?" *Reading World* (March 1978): 256-64.

Hakuta, Kenji, and Cancino, Herlinda. "Trends in Second-Language Acquisition Research." *Harvard Educational Review* 47, no. 3 (1977): 294-316.

Jeffrey, W.E., and Samuels, S.J. "Effect of Method of Reading Training on Initial Learning and Transfer." *Journal of Verbal Learning and Verbal Behavior* 6 (1967): 354-58.

Modiano, Nancy. "National or Mother Language in Beginning Reading: A Comparative Study." *Research in Teaching of English* 11, no. 1 (April 1968): 32-43.

Osterberg, T. *Bilingualism and First School Language.* Urnea: Vasterbottens Tryckeri, 1961.

Schumann, John H. "The Implications of Interlanguage, Pidginization, and Creolization for the Study of Adult Second Language Acquisition." *TESOL Quarterly* 8, no. 2 (June 1974): 145-52.

Selinker, Larry. "Interlanguage." In *International Review of Applied Linguistics and Reading,* edited by Robert E. Schaeffer. Newark, Del.: International Reading Association, 1972.

Sims, Rudine. "Miscue Analysis—Emphasis on Comprehension." In *Applied Linguistics and Reading,* edited by Robert E. Schaeffer. Newark, Del.: International Reading Association, 1979.

Vásquez, James. *Motivation and Chicano Students.* Paper Series of the National Dissemination and Assessment Center, California State University, Los Angeles, Calif., 1978.

Walcutt, Charles; Lamport, J.; and McCracken, G. *Teaching Reading: A Phonic/ Linguistic Approach.* New York: Macmillan, 1974.

The Enactment of Bilingual Education Legislation in Texas: 1969-1973

José E. Vega

Third Place, Outstanding Dissertations
National Advisory Council on Bilingual Education

Degree conferred January 1980
University of Illinois
Champaign, Illinois

Dissertation Committee:
Martin Burlingame, *Chair*
Joel Walters
Gary Orfield
Fred S. Coombs

About the Author

Dr. José E. Vega is an assistant professor of education at the State University of New York College at New Paltz. He has been a member of the Department of Elementary Education since his appointment in 1979. Dr. Vega's responsibilities include teaching, advising undergraduate and graduate students, and working with local parent community organizations. Dr. Vega has taught in elementary school, has been chairman of an adult bilingual education program, and has participated in the organization of conferences on the subjects of bilingual education and the status of Hispanic professionals and students in higher education. Dr. Vega's academic and research interests are in the areas of educational policymaking, sociolinguistics, and teacher training.

SUMMARY

This study was undertaken to identify the factors that may have contributed to the enactment of the Texas Bilingual Education and Training Act in 1973. An examination of the literature on politics and education revealed that little attention had been given to the study of ethnic group politics and its influence on state educational policymaking in the United States.

Meranto's (1967) model for explaining legislative outcomes was used to organize the study. The model called for an examination of the external and internal political changes that occurred at the time the bilingual bill was being considered by the Texas state legislature.

The enactment of bilingual education legislation in Texas was the work of two different legislative sessions. In 1969 the federal bilingual education act provided advocates of bilingual education with legitimate reasons to call for the elimination of restrictive English-only laws and the impetus to pass a permissive bilingual law in Texas. The evidence suggests that, prior to 1969, Chicano legislators and sympathizers could not have proposed the repeal of school language restrictions and have been successful.

When the bilingual bills were introduced by Senator Bernal and Representative Truan the arguments offered in their support were cautious, low-key and well within the acceptable Texas political value system. The evidence suggests that the enactment of the mandatory bilingual education bill in 1973 was attributable to a sympathetic and more liberal legislative body, the expansion of the Texas electorate in 1972, and the Sharpstown political scandal. The involvement of the Texas Association for Continuing Adult Education filled the public advocacy void which neither bilingual educators, Mexican American parents and educators, nor the Texas Education Agency and its officials in the Division of Bilingual Education would or could fill. Through their intense, personal lobbying efforts, they were able to sensitize and favorably influence over half the House members regarding the efficacy of bilingual and adult education programs for Texas.

STATEMENT OF THE PROBLEM

States are increasingly assuming a greater role in educational leadership in the 1980s in support and control of educational reform programs such as bilingual education (Mosher and Wagoner, 1978). Since the enactment of the federal Bilingual Education Act of 1968, twenty-six states have passed similar education laws which either permit or mandate the use of bilingual education instruction for public school children with limited English speaking competence (*A Study of State Programs in Bilingual Education,* 1977). In spite of this continued interest on behalf of linguistically and culturally different children in many states, little research has linked the process of ethnic group political behavior to educational legislative policy outcomes in the states that have enacted such laws.

Why was the first mandatory bilingual education law enacted in Massachusetts and not in Texas? Were the tactics and aims of the various groups who supported this kind of legislation the same or different? How did such things as government structure, attitudes, or the political environment in each state influence the organization and strategy of these pressure groups? What was the nature and extent of federal influence on those states that enacted language education laws? These and other questions dealing with bilingual education interests and policy outcomes have not been examined. The literature of politics and education has given this phenomenon scant attention.

On the other hand, ethnic-group-related politics has been a major theme in political science. In the eastern and northern sections of the United States the persistence of cultural, religious, or linguistic similarities has often been the basis for political organization (Handlin, 1944). The character and persistence of ethnicity in U.S. society has most often been measured in terms of election results and benefits (Bailey and Katz, 1969). Since the early 1920s social scientists were convinced that it was only a matter of time before cultural distinctions based on language, religion, or some other ethnically associated belief system would disappear (Wirth, 1928). Efforts to explain the causes of Black activism and its impact on other minorities during the 1960s, however, challenged the commonly accepted notions on assimilation and political pluralism in U.S. life (Litt, 1970).

Ethnic group politics has been a distinctive feature of Texas political history since the earliest days of the Republic. It has been noted that although Texans have had "little cause to be obsessed about the Negro," as has been the case in Mississippi, "they have been concerned about Mexicans" (Key, 1949, p. 254). Social and political voluntary associations such as the League of United Latin-American Citizens and American G.I. Forum have often played a major role in articulating the concerns and demands of Mexican Americans in Texas since the mid 1920s (García, 1973). Among the many social concerns of Mexican Americans, education has always been given high priority. The need to improve the educational status of Mexican Americans has never been a disputed issue. The differing views regarding the role of language and culture in the public school curriculum, however, have often been the basis for contention between Chicanos and Anglos.

The use of languages other than English as a medium of instruction in U.S. elementary public schools was a common practice dating back to 1926, yet it was not until 1969, after the persistent efforts of two Mexican American legislators, that the Texas legislature authorized the use of a language other than English for instructional purposes. Texas had the greatest number of bilingual programs in the United States prior to 1968, and a considerably long history of bilingual schooling. However, it was not until 1973 that the Texas legislature enacted a mandatory bilingual education law (Zamora, 1977).

The historical evidence suggests that statewide and local politics in Texas has been affected by the ethnic factor. Similarly, ethnic group tactics have been influenced by the political culture of the state. While the ethnic basis for political organizations in northern and eastern states has often been temporary, in Texas the ethnic factor has been a historical phenomenon. Finally, the evidence suggests that the most recent state legislative enactments on behalf of Mexican Americans in Texas have been a reflection of the unique political ambients, as well as an explicit demonstration of the nature and extent of the federal influence.

PURPOSE OF THE STUDY

The purpose of this study was to analyze and describe the genesis and enactment of the Texas Bilingual Education and Training Act of 1973. The study sought to identify the factors that contributed to the passage of this legislation, and to examine the nature and extent of influence that the federal Bilingual Education Act of 1968 may have had on the passage of this state law.

METHODOLOGY

To gain an indepth understanding of how the Texas legislature responded to the demands of Mexican Americans for bilingual education between 1969 and 1973, a historical approach was employed. A historical study of the Texas legislature was used in order to ascertain how such factors as federal initiatives, ethnic demands for educational reform, or changes in the legislature itself affected the enactment of bilingual education legislation in Texas.

CONCEPTUAL FRAMEWORK

The collection, organization, and analysis of the data in this study were generally guided by Easton's general systems approach. Meranto's particular approach to his investigation of the enactment of the Elementary and Secondary Education Act of 1965 was used in this study (Easton, 1957, 1965a, 1965b; Meranto, 1967).

Meranto's model of legislative actions includes two categories of environmental changes: circumstantial conditions and demand articulators. Circumstantial conditions refer to those unexpected changes in the political system that impinge on the policymaking process. Demand articulators identify those actors who directly affect the policymaking process through lobbying, letter writing, and voting. The model also calls for an examination of those changes that occur within the legislature itself. Figure 1 illustrates how some of the data obtained was meaningfully arranged.

The conceptual framework adopted for the study elicited four basic questions that served to guide the direction of the study:

1. What was the nature and extent of the federal government's influence as a circumstantial condition on the legislative process concerning bilingual education?

2. How did other circumstantial changes affect the response of the legislature toward new channels for bilingual education?

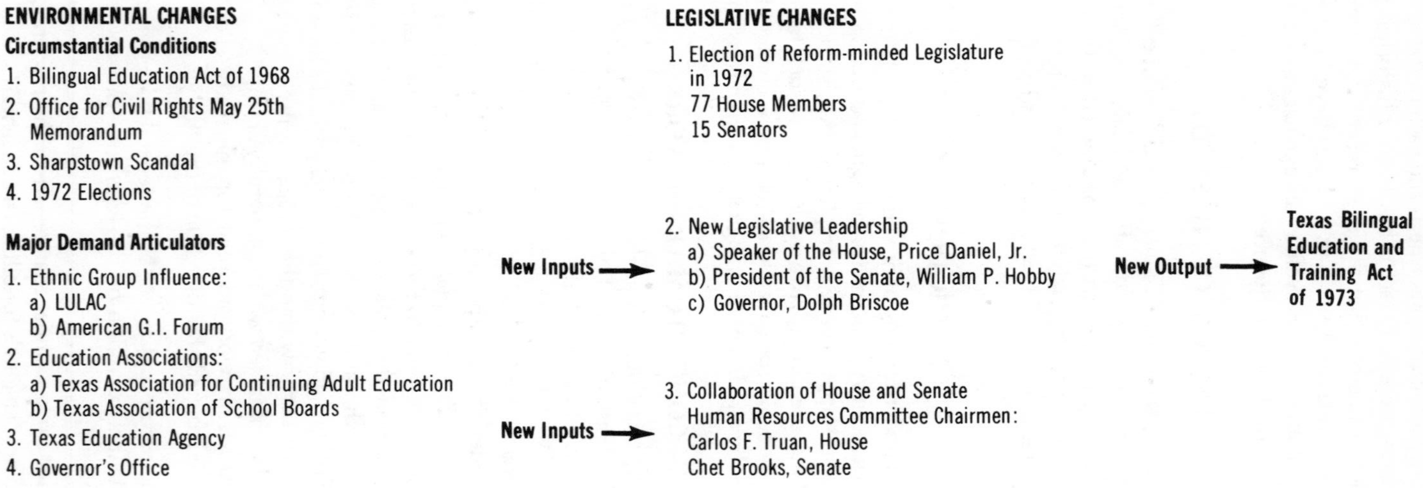

ENVIRONMENTAL CHANGES

Circumstantial Conditions

1. Bilingual Education Act of 1968
2. Office for Civil Rights May 25th Memorandum
3. Sharpstown Scandal
4. 1972 Elections

Major Demand Articulators

1. Ethnic Group Influence:
   a) LULAC
   b) American G.I. Forum
2. Education Associations:
   a) Texas Association for Continuing Adult Education
   b) Texas Association of School Boards
3. Texas Education Agency
4. Governor's Office

New Inputs →

LEGISLATIVE CHANGES

1. Election of Reform-minded Legislature in 1972
   77 House Members
   15 Senators

2. New Legislative Leadership
   a) Speaker of the House, Price Daniel, Jr.
   b) President of the Senate, William P. Hobby
   c) Governor, Dolph Briscoe

3. Collaboration of House and Senate Human Resources Committee Chairmen:
   Carlos F. Truan, House
   Chet Brooks, Senate

New Inputs →

New Output →

Texas Bilingual Education and Training Act of 1973

Figure 1
Model of State Curriculum Policymaking

3. What role did ethnic group leaders and others play as demand articulators in directing the attention of the legislators toward bilingual education?

4. What role did changes in the legislature play in shaping the responses to the demands for bilingual education in the legislative process?

DATA COLLECTION

Pertinent primary and secondary historical documents were examined. These documents included the transcript of the proceedings during the regular legislative sessions as they are recorded in the *House* and *Senate Journals*. Copies of the House and Senate versions of the bilingual bills introduced were reviewed. Transcripts of the official positions and statements of the State Board of Education, which were included in the *Official Agenda,* were examined, and the reports issued by the Texas Education Agency on the subject of bilingual education were read. Reports by other government agencies, position statements made by professional interest groups, and other pertinent documents associated with the passage of the new law were also examined. Secondary sources included some of the state's important newspapers: the *Texas Observer* (Austin), the *Dallas Morning News, Express-News* (San Antonio), and the *Chronicle* (Houston). In addition, articles in national magazines and other newspapers were used for background information.

The major instrument for obtaining information about the events that transpired between 1969 and 1973 was the interview. A few of the key figures in the process were identified in some of the public documents that were reviewed in the early stages of the study. Other leading participants were identified by reputation. Nominations of participants were made by knowledgeable key actors in the decisionmaking process.

Participants were initially contacted by mail. The introductory letter explained the purpose of the study and asked whether the person would be willing to be interviewed. Favorable responses were followed up by telephone calls to determine a convenient place, date, and time during which to conduct the tape-recorded interview.

On several occasions interviews were conducted by telephone with those participants who could not be interviewed in person because of their work schedules and the extra cost involved in having to meet in separate parts of the state. Several of the respondents were interviewed more than once.

Those interviewed included professional educators who were directly involved with lobbying efforts or sought by legislators and state education officials as consultants, legislators and their assistants who sponsored the bilingual bills, spokespersons for different professional lobbying organizations, and the former and current commissioners of education for the state of Texas. Repeated attempts to talk to former governors Preston Smith and

Dolph Briscoe were not successful. However, a telephone interview with one of former Governor Briscoe's administrative assistants was fruitful.

After some of the background information was reviewed and the key participants in the process were identified, questions were developed for the interviews. A semistandardized interview schedule was used. The schedule allowed the interviewer to ask a number of major questions, while at the same time permitting freedom to probe. The major advantage of this kind of interview schedule was that it allowed a certain amount of uniformity, providing the investigator with a standard with which to cross-validate the factual information, recollections, and the different perceptions of the respondents. The possibility of probing respondents was well suited for the case study method, where the main objective was to understand indepth the causes for one particular event (Phillips, 1966).

The following general questions are typical of those that were asked of all the interviewees. Some of the questions were adapted from another case study on the politics of school finance in the state of Wisconsin. The author of the study employed the same conceptual framework to investigate why and how a particular finance bill was enacted (Geske, 1975).

1. Circumstantial Conditions:
   a. What kinds of political changes in Texas prior to 1973 do you think might have aided in the enactment of the Bilingual Education and Training Act?
   b. What kind of influence, if any, do you think the federal government might have had in the enactment of this language-related legislation?

2. Demand Articulators
   a. How did Texas legislators become aware that bilingual instruction in some of its public schools was the best way to meet the educational needs of many Mexican American school children?
   b. Can you recall what kind of role the governor played in endorsing and influencing the passage of the bilingual bill during the Sixty-third Legislature?

3. Legislative Changes:
   a. What legislative factors would you say aided in the passage of the bilingual bill during the sixty-third legislative session in contrast to the two previous legislative sessions?
   b. Can you tell me something about how agreements on particular events were reached?

A complete list of the questions under each of the three categories above is included in the Appendix.

ANALYSIS

A review of the historical data that were collected and examined in the study suggests that the enactment of the Texas Bilingual Education and

Training Act in 1973 was not the result of any single dominant factor. Consequently, it was important to highlight several factors that were found to have had a particular impact on the legislative process. The following factors were examined: the role of the federal government, the function of legislative ambiguity, the primacy of the English language, the support of the governor and ethnic group politics, the support of the speaker, the adult and bilingual education coalition, and the role of the Texas Education Agency.

Federal Role

In 1969 federal initiatives in the area of bilingual education accelerated the slower local pace. The enactment of permissive bilingual education legislation in Texas in 1969 received its major impetus from the enactment of the federal Bilingual Education Act in 1968. Increased federal funding provided local school districts and the Texas Education Agency with a major incentive to participate in another educational program. The federal act provided state advocates with legitimate reasons to ask for the elimination of restrictive language codes. The evidence suggests that prior to 1969 Chicano legislators could not have proposed the repeal of school language restrictions and have been successful. When bills were introduced the arguments were cautious, low-key, and well within the acceptable Texas political value system.

In 1971 Representative Truan's two bills on bilingual education were still optional. The first bill (H.B. 495) was a subdued paraphrase of the May 25 Memorandum, which had been sent to school districts having 5 percent or more national-origin-minority student enrollment the previous year by the U.S. Office of Civil Rights. (That memorandum extended the Civil Rights Act of 1964 to minority language children.) The second bill (H.B. 1024) increased Texas Education Agency (TEA) control over the training of bilingual instructional personnel, the disbursement of funds, and the preparation of teaching materials.

The influence of the federal mandate on the education of linguistically different national-origin-minority schoolchildren on the introduction of bilingual bills in 1973 was even more evident. Senator Brooks's bill (S.B. 121) was heavily influenced by the spirit and language of the May 25 Memorandum. Unlike the bilingual bills that had been introduced during the 62nd legislative session in 1971, this bill was mandatory.

Legislative Ambiguity

The manner in which the first bilingual law was written provides an important insight into the enactment process. The bilingual bills were not as clear statements on all of the objectives of bilingual education as advocates would have preferred. Instead, each bill stressed the importance of English as the primary language of instruction, called for the repeal of certain language restrictions, and gave local districts the option to participate in a new federal education program. According to Rein and White, controversial legislation is very often enacted in this fashion. They noted that at times

> legislation requires ambiguity in the statement of its goals so that coalitions can be formed in support of it, and each group can believe that the legislation serves its own special purposes. (Footnote in Boyd, 1978, p. 584)

It is evident that in Texas legislators viewed the bilingual bills in different ways. Anglo American legislators perceived the bilingual bills as offering a program designed to help poor, non-English-speaking Mexican American schoolchildren to master English. Mexican American advocates of bilingual schooling viewed the passage of bilingual legislation differently. To many the use of Spanish as a medium of instruction was a symbol of prestige and increased social status for the Mexican American in Texas. Often the pedagogical significance of bilingual schooling has been of secondary importance. From the evidence in this study it seems quite clear that arguments that emphasized the advantages of bilingualism and laid claim to legal or human rights would not have successfully convinced Texan legislators.

Mexican American legislators and other advocates of bilingual bicultural education diffused what could have been a highly controversial issue by downplaying the cultural component of the bilingual education bill. The tactic of bilingual advocates in the legislature was to stress the transitional nature of the program by emphasizing the primacy of English.

Primacy of English

It is important to note that major emphasis was given to the primacy of English in each of the bills that were introduced in 1969, 1971, and 1973. In both the permissive and mandatory versions of the bilingual bill, mastery of English by all public school students was declared to be official state policy.

In 1973 the Texas legislature had approved a transitional bilingual education program. It was modeled to a great extent on the bilingual law that had been enacted in Massachusetts the previous year. The objective was to use the children's native language as a medium for classroom instruction while they gradually learned English. The maintenance of linguistic and cultural distinctions was not the law's intended purpose. It is doubtful whether any bill not having a statement on the primacy of English could have been passed. During the House debate on S.B. 121 one of the two last-minute amendments introduced and passed concerned the rightful place of English. It seems clear that state legislators had not approved legal authorization for a bilingual state when they enacted bilingual education laws.

To most of the legislators, problems with English were the root cause for Mexican Americans' low socioeconomic status in Texas. Capitalizing on the business ethos of Texas politics, advocates of adult and bilingual education argued that there was a direct relationship between English language proficiency and economic benefits and productivity.

Governor's Support and Ethnic Group Politics

The role of Governor Dolph Briscoe in the enactment of S.B. 121 was crucial. The newly elected governor delivered on his campaign promises to the Mexican American leadership by requesting over $16 million in new appropriations for the adult and bilingual education bills. The strong and un-expected electoral showing by La Raza Unida party in 1972 was another reason for Briscoe's concern for Mexican Americans. The elections had demonstrated to Democratic party leaders the potential threat that in-dependent Chicano voting could pose to the dominance and stability of the conservative Democratic party.

Bilingual education was a priority of La Raza Unida party platform. By enacting a bilingual education law that benefitted Mexican Americans, the Democratic party weakened the appeal of La Raza Unida, and at the same time helped to strengthen Chicano confidence in the dominant party. The passage of the bilingual education law vindicated the arguments of liberal and conservative Chicanos who chose to work for changes within the system. It seems clear, however, that Chicano political efforts on opposite sides of the ideological spectrum were both instrumental in suggesting immediate legislative considerations on behalf of Mexican Americans in Texas.

Furthermore, the evidence shows that at no time during the advocacy process was the governor made aware of any organized opposition to bilingual education by any influential segment of the Mexican American community. The American G.I. Forum, LULAC, and other Mexican Ameri-can voluntary associations presented a united front on the issue of bilingual instruction in Texas public schools.

Support of the Speaker

Senate Bill 121 had the full support of the leadership in both houses of the legislature. Speaker Price Daniel, Jr.'s support in the House for bilingual education was very important. Without his support it is doubtful the bill would have survived the lengthy debate. Daniel's choices for strategic committee assignments were the key to the bill's success in the House. His appointment of Truan to the influential post of chairman of the Human Resources Committee was a decisive move. In this post Truan was in a much better position to make deals with colleagues in exchange for their votes on the bilingual education bill. The speaker's appointment of sympathetic House members to committees to which the bilingual education bill would be referred for consideration was calculated and deliberate. Speaker Daniel had not forgotten the help that Truan had extended to him in his bid for the leadership of the House. Truan's loyalty and hard work as a member of the "Dirty Thirty" during the Sixty-second Legislature did not go unnoticed or unrewarded.

Adult and Bilingual Education Coalition

In addition to the support that he received from the governor and the speaker of the House, Truan was keenly aware that he also needed some kind of strong, external public support for his bills.

The involvement of the Texas Association for Continuing Adult Education filled the public advocacy void which neither bilingual educators, Mexican American parents and educators, nor the Texas Education Agency and its officials in the Division of Bilingual Education would or could fill. Through their intense, personal lobbying efforts and the barrage of letters that they sent representatives, they were able to sensitize and influence over half the House members on the subjects of bilingual and adult education. The association was not actually concerned with bilingual education per se, but in their minds there was little difference in the goals of each bill. One bill addressed the educational problems of the Mexican American children while the other encompassed the needs of the adults.

The newly elected officers of the association and the two officials in the division of adult continuing education of TEA were goaded by some very practical considerations. They all knew that federal funds for adult education were limited, that the use of these funds was restrictive, and that there was always the threat of these funds' being cut off or decreased. Both the adult and bilingual programs were federally funded. However, the adult education program had been in existence since 1966, whereas the other program had begun only in 1969.

The idea to merge both interests into one concerted legislative strategy that would assure the enactment of both bills came from Representative Truan. In Truan's mind both bills were policies that needed to be "sold" to his colleagues in the House and Senate. One bill ensured that Mexican American children in the primary grades would not have to fail because of linguistic limitations or negative self-concepts. The other bill ensured that the parents of these children were no longer denied the opportunity that they were not given in their youth.

The Texas Education Agency

From 1968 to 1972 the Texas Education Agency acted as a facilitator and responded to external demands for change which emanated from within the state or from Washington, D.C. The agency provided a formal, structural link between the Mexican American community and the legislature.

Formal linkages, however, were not enough to assure the passage of new and controversial education legislation. Between 1969 and 1973 the agency never actively lobbied for the enactment of any of its new proposals. The bilingual and adult education bills were no exception. The agency made its formal requests for legislative consideration of both bills as prescribed by law, but personnel in the bilingual education division of the agency did not actively push for their passage or funding. With the exception of Bob G. Allen and Manuel Garza, TEA officials did not actively lobby for the enactment of either bill.

The agency's failure to push for the passage of its legislative recommendations was rooted in its image as an impartial, professional, and nonpolitical organization, obedient and subservient to the expressed will of the people of Texas through its elected lawmakers.

CONCLUSION

Although the need, the interest, and much of the early expertise and support for bilingual education came from Texas, it was not the first state to enact a mandatory bilingual education law. The advocates of bilingual education legislation were successful in articulating their demands for educational change at the federal level before they were able to influence the passage of similar state legislation. In general, the evidence obtained in this study suggests that the enactment of bilingual education legislation in Texas in 1969 and in 1973 was influenced by Mexican American demands for innovations in the state's public school curriculum. In addition, the evidence demonstrates that the strategy and tactics that Mexican American legislators adopted to pass the bilingual education bills were a reflection of the political context, as it was an explicit illustration of the nature and extent of the federal influence on state educational policymaking.

Notwithstanding the above factors, the evidence strongly suggests that the most important factor in accounting for the successful passage of the Texas bilingual education law seems to have been the role of the powerful Speaker of the House. Without his active support the bilingual bill could never have been passed by the Sixty-third Texas Legislature in 1973.

It took four years to enact a mandatory bilingual education law in Texas. Incremental and nonincremental educational policymaking went on simultaneously. The push for enacting a bilingual education law was low keyed. Earlier legislative successes, and possibly the passage of similar laws in other states, served to broaden the demands of Mexican Americans for the enactment of bilingual education legislation in 1973.

Finally, the study suggests that Mexican American demands for bilingual bicultural schooling were partly the result of a long history of educational neglect. Segregated schools, serious financial disparities among school districts, and the indifference and prejudice of the majority culture compounded a problem that should have been more seriously addressed by local and state public officials.

APPENDIX

INTERVIEW SCHEDULE

I. CIRCUMSTANTIAL CONDITIONS:

1. In your opinion, did federal initiatives in the area of bilingual education have any influence on the enactment of the Texas Bilingual Education and Training Act of 1973?

2. Can you recall specific political events prior to 1973 which may have influenced the introduction and successful passage of the Bilingual Education and Training Act during the Sixty-third Texas Legislature?

3. As far as you can remember what effect did such court cases as *United States* v. *Texas* (1971) or *San Antonio I.S.D.* v. *Rodríguez* (1973) have on the enactment of the Bilingual Education and Training Act of 1973?

4. In your opinion, would the Bilingual Education and Training Act of 1973 have been enacted if its implementation depended on an increase in new taxes for the state of Texas at the time that it was enacted?

5. What kind of influence do you think the HEW Memorandum of May 25, 1970, which called for school districts to take affirmative steps to rectify the language deficiency of many national-origin-minority group children, may have had on the enactment of bilingual education legislation during the Sixty-third Texas Legislature in 1973?

II. DEMAND ARTICULATORS:

1. During the past ten years, in what ways has your organization supported bilingual education efforts in the state of Texas?

2. Has your organization always favored bilingual education instruction for Mexican American students? If not, what was your earlier position? Why did you change?

3. What role did your organization play in influencing the enactment of the Texas Bilingual Education and Training Act of 1973?

4. Can you recall how the need for bilingual instruction for a great number of Mexican Americans who attended Texas public schools came to your attention?

5. What rationale, evidence, or group prompted you to recommend the establishment of a bilingual education program in your outgoing address to the Sixty-third Texas Legislature in 1973?

6. What prompted you to recommend the establishment of "an adequate bilingual education program" in your address to the Sixty-third Legislature?

7. Under what conditions would you have vetoed the bilingual education bill which was enacted (S.B. 121) during the Sixty-third Legislature?

8. What prompted the Texas Education Agency to recommend the establishment of a bilingual education program in 1970 and again in 1972?

9. Had there been any earlier attempts to recommend the establishment of a mandatory bilingual education law in Texas?

10. In addition to the governor and legislature, were there specific legislators to whom these recommendations were made?

11. In your opinion, what conditions do you think prevented the establishment of a bilingual education program by the Sixty-second Legislature in 1971?

12. Can you remember what part the Texas Education Agency played in influencing the enactment of H.B. 103, Chapter 289, a law permitting bilingual instruction up to the 6th grade and beyond, with TEA approval, during the Sixty-first Legislature in 1969?

III. LEGISLATIVE CHANGES:

1. Can you recall any legislative changes during the Sixty-third Legislature which may have had a bearing on the enactment and passage of the Texas Bilingual Education and Training Act of 1973?

2. As far as you can remember, what effect did the election results in the autumn of 1972 have on the enactment of the Bilingual Education and Training Act of 1973?

3. Can you recall what kind of role the governor played in endorsing and influencing the passage of the bilingual education bill during the Sixty-third Legislature?

4. In your opinion, did the Texas Education Agency play an important advocacy role in influencing the enactment of the Bilingual Education and Training Act of 1973?

5. Can you remember what groups, consultants, or other sources of information enabled you to form a favorable opinion about the effectiveness and purpose of bilingual instruction?

6. Can you recall any one particular reason or evidence which convinced you about the merits of the bilingual education bill that was proposed in 1973?

7. In your opinion, why do you think a bilingual education law had not been enacted prior to 1973?

8. In your opinion, what events or conditions outside of the legislature may have accounted for the passage of the bilingual education bill during the Sixty-third Legislature?

9. How did you become aware that bilingual instruction was what your constituents wanted?

10. In your opinion, would the enactment of the Bilingual Education and Training Act of 1973 have been possible without the passage of similar legislation at the federal level?

11. Can you remember any attempt to introduce a bill that would have permitted the use of language other than English as a legitimate medium of instruction in the public schools as early as 1967 during the Sixtieth Legislature?

REFERENCES

Bailey, Harry A., and Katz, Ellis, eds. *Ethnic Group Politics.* Columbus, Ohio: Charles E. Merrill, 1969.

Boyd, William Lowe. "The Changing Politics of Curriculum Policy-Making for American Schools." *Review of Educational Research* 48, no. 4 (Fall 1978): 577-628.

Development Associates, Inc. "A Final Report on Their Status." *A Study of State Programs in Bilingual Education.* Supporting Volumes I-IV. Washington, D.C.: Development Associates, Inc., March 1977.

Easton, David. "An Approach to the Analysis of Political Systems." *World Politics* 9 (April 1957): 383-400.

_____ . *A Framework for Political Analysis.* Englewood Cliffs, N.J.: Prentice-Hall, 1965a.

_____ . *A Systems Analysis of Political Life.* New York: John Wiley and Sons, 1965b.

García, Chris. *Political Socialization of Chicano Children.* New York: Praeger, 1973.

Geske, Terry G. "The Politics of Reforming School Finance in Wisconsin." Ph.D. dissertation, University of Wisconsin, 1975.

Handlin, Oscar. "The Immigrant and American Politics." In *Foreign Influences in American Life,* edited by David F. Bowers. Princeton: Princeton University Press, 1944.

Key, V.O., Jr., *Southern Politics in State and Nation.* New York: Alfred A. Knopf, 1949.

Litt, Edgar. *Ethnic Politics in American Life.* Glenview, Ill.: Scott, Foresman, 1970.

Meranto, Philip. *The Politics of Federal Aid to Education in 1965: A Study in Political Innovation.* Syracuse: Syracuse University Press, 1967.

Mosher, Edith K., and Wagoner, Jennings L., Jr., eds. *The Changing Politics of Education.* Berkeley, Calif.: McCutchan Publishing Corporation, 1978.

Phillips, Bernard S. *Social Research.* New York: The MacMillan Company, 1966.

Wirth, Louis. *The Ghetto.* Chicago: Chicago University Press, 1928.

Zamora, Jesús Ernesto. "A Survey of Texas' Bilingual-Bicultural Education Programs." Ph.D. dissertation, The University of Texas at Austin, 1977.

Evaluation into Policy:
Bilingual Education, 1978

Iris Polk Berke

Semifinalist, Outstanding Dissertations
National Advisory Council on Bilingual Education

Degree conferred June 1980
Stanford University School of Education
Stanford, California

Dissertation Committee:
Michael W. Kirst, *Chair*
Robert L. Politzer
Lee J. Cronbach

About the Author

Dr. Iris Polk Berke is Staff Assistant/Evaluator with the Santa Clara County (Calif.) Office of Education. She has served as a consultant to the California State Department of Education and the California Educational Management and Evaluation Commission, and as a research assistant for the Stanford University Teacher Corps Project. Her publications include articles on educational evaluation and community involvement in education.

SUMMARY

This study was undertaken to investigate the influence of the American Institutes for Research (AIR) *Evaluation of the Impact of the ESEA Title VII Spanish/English Bilingual Education Program* (1978) on the 1978 reauthorization of the Bilingual Education Act. The study traced policy development through ten executive agency (HEW) units and the congressional authorization and appropriations process to passage of the Education Amendments of 1978. The kinds of policy developed at each step and how such policy was influenced by the AIR evaluation findings are described.

The major study findings were:

1. The existence of several units within the executive agency (HEW) devoted to commissioning and analyzing evaluations guarantees the incorporation of such findings into formal policymaking procedures.

2. Various executive agency units used the AIR findings differently and selectively, depending on their normal policy functions.

3. The bilingual education program received negative attention in a *60 Minutes* broadcast, a *Washington Post* feature article by Noel Epstein, and the AIR evaluation. To counter this, program advocates marshalled evidence of program success. These activities increased the evidence brought to bear on formal bilingual education policy development within government.

4. The executive branch gave greater weight to the AIR evaluation findings than Congress. Congress was more skeptical of evaluation, and placed greater weight on constituent support of the program.

STATEMENT OF THE PROBLEM

Use of Federal Evaluation for Policymaking

Federal program evaluation has become a major enterprise. In 1979, the U.S. Department of Health, Education, and Welfare (HEW) requested more than $100 million for education program evaluation and research (*Senate Hearings*, p. 842). The use of this research and evaluation for policymaking is complex and poorly understood. Further investigation of the ways in which program evaluation is used in the federal education policy process is warranted.

Literature on the use of social science by policymakers provides a framework for understanding the use of evaluation. There are multiple "uses," described by Weiss (1977), Ewing (1977), Caplan (1975), and Rich (1977). Listing such uses helps conceptualize the problem of how evaluation findings are used for policymaking. What is needed next is a detailed description of *how* such use occurs. While individual decisions are often thought to represent "policy," this study adopts a broader definition:

> . . . Decisions are not the same thing as policy. Part of what is meant by social policy is a system of knowledge and beliefs—ideas about the causes of social problems, assumptions about how society works and notions about appropriate solutions. (Cohen and Garet, 1975, p. 21)

55

Many kinds of policy are made by many actors at various levels of government in both the executive and legislative branches. There are formal, predictable cycles for much federal policy development, but some policy is influenced by factors outside the formal routines. Before one can understand how evaluation is used in the policy process, one must thoroughly understand federal education policymaking.

PURPOSE OF THE STUDY: HOW DID THE FINDINGS OF THE AIR IMPACT EVALUATION INFLUENCE 1978 REAUTHORIZATION OF ESEA, TITLE VII?

To investigate how an evaluation influences policy, this study traced the use of one evaluation's findings for an eighteen-month period that culminated in the 1978 legislative reauthorization of the Bilingual Education Act. The evaluation received considerable attention. The interim findings were available eighteen months before scheduled reauthorization, which provided ample time for the findings to be incorporated into routine policy procedures. The $2 million AIR *Evaluation of the Impact of the Spanish/English Title VII Bilingual Education Program* was a major undertaking intended to be used in formulating policy for the bilingual education program. This study tried to determine exactly how this evaluation's findings influenced the 1978 reauthorization of the Title VII Program.

THEORETICAL FRAMEWORK: USE OF SOCIAL SCIENCE FOR POLICYMAKING

This analysis provides concrete information to support generalizations in the existing literature on the use of research and evaluation for policymaking. Most prior work in this area, done by Caplan, Weiss, and Rich, used surveys of policymakers in many governmental agencies. Caplan (1975) found that scientific information merges with and becomes indistinguishable from other kinds of policy inputs, that it is difficult to trace consequences of such information because it usually has more than one effect, and that there is no single way to assess the impact of social science findings on national policymaking. Rich (1977) distinguishes between short-term use for policy *action* and long-term use for gaining a better *understanding* of the policy context. Weiss (1977) lists many uses of research: instrumental uses for problem-solving, knowledge-driven uses, interactive uses to reconceptualize policy issues, such as for political ammunition, and a variety of miscellaneous uses—e.g., delaying action, avoiding responsibility for making a decision, winning recognition for a successful program, maintaining government prestige for supporting well-known researchers, etc. This study of the influence of the AIR *Impact Evaluation* on the 1978 reauthorization of Title VII examines whether and how these generalizations apply in this particular case.

METHODOLOGY

This case study of the influence of an evaluation on program policy used the methods of historical and policy research. The research relied on considerable background reading and experience in the areas of bilingual education, language acquisition, evaluation utilization, federal policymaking, and the ESEA, Title VII bilingual education program. To understand the Title VII program thoroughly, the author visited bilingual classes and read prior program evaluations, General Accounting Office (GAO) studies, past and current legislation, books, journal articles, and newspaper analyses of the program. He studied the AIR interim and final reports, and interviewed the AIR project director, Malcolm Danoff, and members of the evaluation staff. To gain a thorough understanding of the federal education policy process, the author read widely on passage of specific legislation, implementation of programs, federal education policy, and political science.

To investigate the use of the AIR Impact Evaluation for Title VII's 1978 reauthorization, the author interviewed many people from relevant executive agency units, congressional committees, interest groups, and the media, and gathered documents that trace the development of Title VII's 1978 reauthorization policy. The study is a step-by-step account of:

1. The usual functions of governmental units that make and affect bilingual education policy

2. The use of research findings by those units

3. The influence of the AIR findings on the 1978 reauthorization of the Bilingual Education Act.

The techniques of historical and policy research were used to collect and analyze the information. Different information sources were used for different aspects of the study. The most relevant and available sources were used. In the executive agency (HEW), where much documentation is for use only *within* the agency, personal interviews provided considerable information. Conversely, Congress documents its activities thoroughly in hearings, successive versions of legislation, committee reports, and the *Congressional Record.* Very few congressional staff people and no members of Congress were available for interviews. Therefore, the section on congressional policy development relies heavily on public documents, whereas the section on executive agency policy development was augmented by personal interviews. Sources are clearly indicated throughout the study.

Each governmental unit that played an important role in developing Title VII reauthorization policy was studied. In the executive branch, the investigation begins at the Office of Bilingual Education, and progresses through Education Division and HEW units (Office of Bilingual Education, Office of Planning, Budget and Evaluation: Budget and Evaluation, National Center for Education Statistics, National Institute of Education, Office of the Commissioner/Policy Studies, the Assistant Secretary for

Education, the HEW Assistant Secretary for Education Legislation, the HEW Assistant Secretary for Planning and Evaluation, and the Secretary of Health, Education, and Welfare). Executive policymaking culminated in the development of the administration proposals for ESEA of 1978. The study then follows congressional policy development from House and Senate authorization and appropriations committees, to the floor of the House and Senate, through conferences, and passage of the Education Amendments of 1978. The case study describes the kinds of policy developed at each step, and how such policy was influenced by the AIR evaluation findings.

FINDINGS

Certain characteristics of the political climate, the bilingual education program, and the AIR impact evaluation itself contributed to the evaluation's role in determining 1978 reauthorization policy. The Education Amendments of 1978 were developed in a climate of fiscal and political conservatism. California had just passed Proposition 13, and there was considerable pressure to "trim fat" in government. The Great Society programs of the 1960s were increasingly expected to prove their worth. A widely read *Washington Post* journalist, Noel Epstein, questioned whether it was appropriate for the federal government to support language and cultural maintenance. President Carter favored an English as a second language (ESL) approach to teaching English to speakers of other languages. He opposed multicultural and bilingual approaches. This was not a favorable climate for bilingual education.

The bilingual education program is highly controversial and lacking in political clout. It is not a favored program in the executive bureaucracy. Bilingual education funds have been distributed by competitive grants unlike most education funds, which have been distributed by formula. The lack of a distribution formula subjected bilingual education funds to occasional intrusion from outside the Office of Bilingual Education; the Secretary of HEW tried to reallocate Title VII funds to districts that did not qualify under normal procedures. The program suffered from less-than-equal protection in the executive agency. These factors suggest that negative attention to the program will lead to policy action to "fix up" the program, and that such efforts would meet with little resistance within the bureaucracy.

The AIR interim findings were available at a crucial time in the reauthorization process. The findings were extremely negative, and were supported by other evidence (a GAO report, medium attention, departmental and congressional concern about the program). Powerful people had a stake in the evaluation. The negative attention eventually led to a reaction on the part of program advocates. Whereas the AIR findings were accepted by some actors in the policy process, others staunchly refuted them. Researchers pointed out that the evaluation methodology was open to criticism, and the conclusions were subject to differing interpretations. Controversy over the evaluation findings increased the evidence brought to bear on the reauthorization process. The quantity of evidence considered reduced the likelihood that any one source of information would be unduly influential. In the executive agency, this served to whet the desire for even more information on which to base policy recommendations. In Congress, however, conflicting interpretations of the evaluation findings confirmed congressional skepticism of research. Congressional reauthorization placed considerably less weight on the evaluation findings than did executive branch reauthorization policy.

The AIR evaluation played a catalytic role in the 1978 reauthorization of ESEA, Title VII. Unusual media attention to the bilingual education program and the evaluation findings aroused public concern. This concern assured that the program would be carefully scrutinized during the reauthorization process. Thus, the informal or extra-governmental influences of the media and public concern affected formal governmental policy processes by increasing the number of participants at the information-gathering stage, and by expanding the evidence brought to bear on Title VII reauthorization policy development.

INFLUENCE OF THE AIR EVALUATION FINDINGS

The AIR findings were used selectively and differently by various executive agency units, Congress, the media, and interest groups. As a result of the AIR impact evaluation, the Office of Bilingual Education management procedures were "tightened." The OE Evaluation Office (OPBE-Evaluation) has reduced emphasis on commissioning impact evaluations that rely heavily on experimental or quasi-experimental design. The OE Budget Office (OPBE-Budget) requested no increase in funding for direct service to bilingual education projects because the AIR evaluation questioned the efficacy of the program. The Budget Office instead sought a $10 million increase for research in bilingual education to answer some of the many questions raised by the AIR evaluation and subsequent departmental scrutiny of the program. The culmination of executive branch Title VII reauthorization policy, the administration proposals for 1978 reauthorization of Title VII, sought:

1. Clearer targeting criteria, aimed at teaching English to the neediest children

2. A five-year limit on funding individual projects

3. A 300 percent increase in funding for research in bilingual education.

These recommendations went to Congress, which responded to a different set of pressures than the administration. In Congress, pressure to support the program outweighed pressure to "tighten it up." Thus, congressional reauthorization of Title VII essentially overturned the administration's recommendations to target the program on the neediest children, limit the length of time a local district may receive funds, and greatly expand the research effort in bilingual education.

In the executive branch, individual sources of information are analyzed, processed, and amalgamated by staff members into increasingly concise "policy-relevant information." High-level policymakers rarely deal with raw information; they select among already formulated policy options. Thus, the influence of evaluation findings is largely dependent on staff interpretation. In this case, the close scrutiny of the bilingual education program during reauthorization led to reconceptualization of the policy issues underlying the program. For the first time, serious discussion was devoted to changing the delivery system from discretionary grants to an entitlement formula. Thus, the evaluation served as a catalyst for increasing the seriousness of reauthorization policy development. The policy process considered all points of view, and the resulting reauthorization did not proceed in a direct line from the AIR evaluation findings to development of bilingual education policy. The findings did influence the outcome, but probably caused more constituent support for the program to be brought into policy deliberations than might have occurred in the absence of negative evaluation findings.

CONCLUSION

The work of Weiss, Caplan, and Rich in evaluation utilization for policy-making was borne out by the study. There were multiple uses of the AIR evaluation findings by policymakers; the findings were used differently by various organizational units in HEW and in Congress, and the findings were used in combination with other sources of information. Media attention to the bilingual education program and the evaluation findings assured close scrutiny of the program during reauthorization policy development. Short-term reactive policies were developed to "do something" immediately. When the media attention had died down, those policies were gradually countered by more carefully considered, long-term program policy. The reauthorization process led to a sharpening of the program's goals, but many of the policies developed work against implementation of those goals.

The case study highlighted the constellation of circumstances (media attention, timing, questionable evaluation methodology, controversial program, differences between administration and congressional policy concerns) that influenced how the AIR findings affected Title VII's 1978 reauthorization. Rather atypical circumstances drew attention to the bilingual education program and the AIR impact evaluation prior to reauthorization. This attention guaranteed careful analysis in the executive branch and Congress. Thus, the evaluation served to increase the intensity and breadth of evidence brought to bear on bilingual education policy development.

IMPLICATIONS OF THE STUDY

This case study of the influence of the AIR Impact Evaluation on Title VII reauthorization in 1978 described the many stages of the policy process, the actors, and the outcome. It showed that "policy" is fluid, and that there are many ways in which to influence policy. It is important for people who have a stake in particular policies to understand the process and know how to influence it to increase the likelihood that their preferences will prevail. The study underscored the importance of vocal constituent support for the bilingual education program, even in the face of powerful negative criticism and administration efforts to "tighten up" the program. The study emphasizes the importance of program advocates being in very close touch with policymakers at all steps of the process, and of knowing what is happening at all times. In this way, they can maximize the possibility of participating in decisions that will affect the bilingual education program. As the study showed, there are many, many areas of policy influence—evaluation, research, budget, targeting, parent involvement, training, distribution of funds, etc.—all of which are subject to a variety of influences. The more constituents know about what policies are subject to manipulation, and how to bring about certain kinds of change, the more effective they will be in affecting those changes themselves.

REFERENCES

American Institutes for Research. *Study Design and Interim Findings.* Evaluation of the Impact of ESEA Title VII Spanish/English Bilingual Education Program, vol. I. Palo Alto, Calif.: American Institutes for Research, 1977.

_____ . *Year Two Impact Data, Education Processes, and In-Depth Analyses.* Evaluation of the Impact of ESEA Title VII Spanish/English Bilingual Education Program, vol. III. Palo Alto, Calif.: American Institutes for Research, 1978.

Caplan, Nathan; Morrison, Andrea; and Stambaugh, Russell J. *The Use of Social Science Knowledge in Policy Decisions at the National Level: A Report to Respondents.* Ann Arbor, Mich.: Institute for Social Research, 1975.

CBS. "Why Johnny Can't Read." *60 Minutes,* 26 Feb. 1978.

Cohen, David K., and Garet, Michael S. "Reforming Educational Policy with Applied Social Science." *Harvard Educational Review* 45 (Feb. 1975): 17-43.

Epstein, Noel. "The Bilingual Battle: Should Washington Finance Ethnic Identities?" *Washington Post,* 5 June 1977, p.C1.

Ewing, Blair. "Report of Working Panel III: Improving the Utilization of Evaluation Findings. In *Proceedings of a Symposium on the Use of Evaluation by Federal Agencies,* vol. 1, edited by Eleanor Chelimsky, McLean Va.: The Mitre Corporation, 1977.

Rich, Robert. "Uses of Social Science Information by Federal Bureaucrats: Knowledge for Action vs. Knowledge for Understanding." In *Using Social Research in Public Policy Making,* edited by Carol H. Weiss. Lexington, Mass.: D.C. Heath & Co., 1977.

U.S., *Senate Hearings before the Committee on Appropriations.* Departments of Labor and Health, Education, and Welfare and Related Agencies Appropriations Fiscal Year 1979. 95th Congress, Second Session, Part 3: Education Programs. Washington, D.C.: U.S. Government Printing Office, 1978.

Weiss, Carol H., ed. *Using Social Research in Public Policy Making.* Lexington, Mass.: D.C. Heath & Co., 1977.

A Sociological Case Study of Bilingual Education and Its Effects on the Schools and the Community

Virginia Parker Collier

Semifinalist, Outstanding Dissertations
National Advisory Council on Bilingual Education

Degree conferred July 1980
University of Southern California School of Education
Los Angeles, California

Dissertation Committee:
Henry D. Acland, *Chair*
Carlos J. Ovando
Eugène J. Brière

About the Author

Dr. Virginia Parker Collier is Assistant Professor of Education and Associate Director for Bilingual/Multicultural Education at George Mason University. She was previously instructor in bilingual/multicultural education at Trinity College in Washington, D.C., and a teaching assistant in ESL at the University of Southern California's American Language Institute. She has also been a bilingual/ESL teacher in the District of Columbia public schools. Dr. Collier has written *On Bilingual Classrooms* with Carlos Ovando, to be published in 1982.

SUMMARY

This study was designed to examine the complexities of implementation of bilingual bicultural education and its effects on both the community and the schools. The Washington, D.C. bilingual program was chosen as a manageable unit for this ethnographic study, as it serves a small, heterogeneous population using a variety of models of bilingual education in eleven elementary and three secondary schools.

The case study description provides details of administrative decisions and negotiations, federal influence, bilingual teachers' and counselors' perceptions, relationships between bilingual and regular school staff, parent and community involvement in schools, effects on students as perceived by adults connected to the program, and Hispanic and Chinese community development, from 1970 to 1980.

One overall theme of the analysis focuses on the gradual emergence of the Hispanic community as an identified political factor in the schools and the wider community. The second theme examines the change process within schools created by the bilingual innovation. This case study illustrates the importance of holistic study for a fuller examination of the complexity of school programs, rather than relying on narrow evaluations that only stress student outcomes as a measurement of the success or failure of a school program.

BACKGROUND AND STATEMENT OF THE PROBLEM

Bilingual bicultural education[1] as it has developed in the United States in the last two decades is highly political and complicated to implement. As the most recent educational strategy for students of limited English proficiency, models of implementation have increased in complexity as federal and state legislation and court orders have mandated or encouraged some form of bilingual education. After projects are begun, refunding decisions become highly politicized as target constituency groups become advocates and monolingual, assimilationist opposition groups form. Deep-seated questions are raised in debates in legislatures as to whether it is the role of federal and state governments to encourage a culturally pluralistic society or to follow the pattern of the early twentieth century of assimilation through immersion into the dominant mainstream.

Yet those committed to bilingual education claim that it is worth the pains of implementation: it provides an optimal environment for learning a

---

[1]Throughout this study, the shortened term *bilingual education* is used to refer to bilingual bicultural education. Without going into detail on the controversy surrounding the relationship between language and culture, it is assumed in this study that culture is an integral part of language and is expressed in many ways through the vehicle of language. Therefore, *bilingual education* implies that bicultural teaching is an integral component of any instruction given in two languages.

second language, for both students of limited English proficiency and English speakers (Dulay and Burt, 1976); it enhances self-concept for students of minority status in the society (Troike, 1978); a two-way model including English speakers provides for learning in an integrated, equal-status setting (Fishman, 1976); and bilingual education provides an avenue for closer school-community relations (Read, Spolsky, and Neundorf, 1976). These affirmations concerning the effects of bilingual education in the United States are like articles of faith; they have a small empirical base. Researchers are just beginning to examine seriously some of the most basic questions. In an emerging field[2] with this type of complexity, holistic studies are useful in shedding light on the nature of an innovation and providing insight into research questions for future studies.

To date, a very limited number of studies have examined the total context of a bilingual program. Most of the studies available at this time are program evaluations. Federal- and state-required evaluations tend to place emphasis on measurement of short-term outcomes, such as student achievement; yet research on bilingual education in other countries has concluded that only longitudinal studies of at least three to four years in a stable program demonstrate the effectiveness of bilingual education (Swain, 1979; Tucker, 1980). An equally serious limitation of current evaluation practices is the emphasis on measurement of the effectiveness of the policymakers' goals, rather than examination of broader sociocultural dimensions that consider the total context of the school environment, including its relationship to the community (Spolsky, 1978).

Therefore, the approach to this research is in the form of a sociological case study of one particular school innovation, the bilingual program of the Washington, D.C. public schools. This study has been carried out to shed light on the complexities of implementation of bilingual bicultural education and its effects on both the community and the schools. The study was born out of the researcher's intimate knowledge of the Washington, D.C. bilingual program as a parent and teacher over a five-year period and grew through physical separation from the program with two years of reading and reflection on that experience. The research culminated in sixteen months of total immersion in the setting through observation of school and community activities; data collection from Bilingual Office and community files, the Census Bureau, administrative offices of the D.C. public schools, and the local media; and 204 formal and informal interviews with randomly selected participants among Hispanic, Chinese, and English-speaking bilingual and regular school staff and community members.

---

[2]Bilingual education is "new" only for the United States in modern decades in the public schools. It has been in existence in countries all over the world for centuries. In the United States, instruction in languages other than English was used in public schools during the nineteenth century, and there have always been bilingual schools in the private sector (Fishman, 1966, 1976).

The research design of this study has been guided and influenced by anthropological and sociological descriptions and analyses of schools such as those by Hargreaves (1967), Kleinfeld (1979), Levy (1970), Modiano (1973), Ogbu (1974), Peshkin (1978), Philips (1970), Rosenfeld (1971), Spindler (1974), and Wolcott (1973, 1977). These studies attempt to tell a whole story by being inclusive rather than narrowly focusing on individual variables. They try to capture several levels of reality in all their complexity, through examination of unintentional as well as conscious goals and outcomes of schooling. Similarly, this study describes many levels of reality as perceived by the adults who participated in or were affected by this school innovation, and the analysis examines conscious, changing, and unconscious processes taking place.

OVERVIEW OF CASE STUDY DESCRIPTION

The overall focus of the study centers around how change occurs in a school system and its impact on the community. Within this focus, two broad themes are developed: the gradual maturation of the D.C. Hispanic community and its relationship to the public schools, and the process of change within schools. The case study description begins with background information on the Hispanic community and the D.C. public schools in the mid-1960s, as each is perceived by Hispanics and school personnel involved in public school politics of that time. The reader is introduced to the process through which the idea of bilingual education evolved, the early stages of adaptation of bilingual staff to the school system and the resistance of regular staff, and the gradual evolution of a complex and expanding innovation. The emerging Hispanic community is described, along with its close connections with the D.C. bilingual program. Parent and community participation in schools is analyzed with focus on the Hispanic community, although some of the impact on Chinese and English-speaking parents is also described. A shift away from innovation and toward institutionalization of the program is increasingly evident as federal funding adds more office staff positions, beginning in 1974, and federal legislation and court decisions influence the course of the school reform. The analysis ends with the school year 1979-1980, with all bilingual positions supported by federal funds absorbed into the local school budget.

ANALYSIS AND FINDINGS

Throughout the case study description, analysis is woven into the story. One overall theme of the analysis focuses on the change process within schools. Whereas the literature on institutional change generally has examined the goals of federal or centralist planners and measured the implementation process by fidelity to the original goals combined with adaptation to the local school system (Farrar, DeSanctis, and Cohen, 1979; Rand, 1974–1977), this study extends the change literature through focus less on an original plan and more on a complex view of evolution of a program in response to multiple changing local and federal influences. None of the observed changes in schools in this study can be seen as linear progressions from A to B; rather, change is seen as the creative use of conflict between A and B, here labeled unresolved tensions, which emerge, disappear, reappear, or find new manifestations in the course of evolution of the bilingual program.

The subtheme which best captures this characteristic of change is the tension between a desire to remain innovative, flexible, and charismatic, and to prod the local school system from outside, on the one hand, and the need to institutionalize the program, which is associated with bureaucratization and standardization, on the other. Additional subthemes which exhibit similar characteristics are the unresolved tensions between continuing flexibility in teaching methods and use of materials, and the push for standardization through curriculum writing and testing; between the reality of constantly expanding, shifting, never-ending problems, and the desire to solve one fixed, predefined problem; between informality and professionalism; between democratic decisionmaking and authoritarian patterns; between deep concern for and direct involvement with students in schools, and office isolation from school problems; between pressing for new rules for international students and accepting the system's rules; and between the desire for cohesion among staff and the development of professional distance. This study illustrates how both sides of each tension manifest themselves in a variety of ways throughout the nine years covered in the research. These tensions are not seen as problems to be solved but as sources of constructive and unending, complex change.

This kind of unresolved tension may especially characterize the nature of bilingual education because of the many inherent conflicts the innovation is intended to address in the United States. For example, in Washington, D.C., the informal knowledge among bilingual staff exists that the full, two-way maintenance bilingual education has been highly successful in student achievement and attitudes, with full equal-status integration of both Hispanics and English speakers. Yet the reality of small numbers of Spanish speakers in other schools necessitates providing only transitional bilingual and English as a second language (ESL) services, which are regarded by staff and students as a lower-status, compensatory program with somewhat limited success. The same tension exists in bilingual education viewed from the federal level. Goals of bilingual programs are frequently broadly stated and unspecific because they reflect the value conflicts inherent in the legislation and program guidelines, which in turn reflect legitimate differences and conflicts within the broader society itself (Marsh, Cassidy, and Mora, 1980).

The second theme of this case study focuses on the maturation of the Hispanic community and its relationship to the public schools. Within this theme, the following issues come into the discussion and analysis: the process of emerging leadership within a small, new, maturing, urban ethnic community; use of the schools as one vehicle for community empowerment and consciousness raising; negotiations between groups for control of schools in a pluralistic urban setting; and the process of greater parent participation in schools and the limits of parental involvement in decisionmaking.

Over the ten years covered by the study, many changes have taken place within the D.C. Hispanic community. It has moved from early experimental, haphazard efforts at community organization to the present, more organized, but democratically expanded, base for decisionmaking in the community. Even though the Hispanic community is relatively small, Hispanics have made considerable progress toward becoming a working, effective, politically visible, lively force within the total D.C. community. This study found that the public schools have served an important function in this process of community development. Members of the Hispanic community were able to use the schools as one means of providing support for a sense of community identity. They then built upon that raised consciousness to make full use of a minority community's rights within this society.

The bilingual program was an integral part of this process through roles played by the school-community coordinator and bilingual counselors, actual hiring of Spanish-speaking bilingual staff and teacher aides, close contact with and leadership in the Hispanic community, parental training, and many structures for direct parental involvement in schools. The even smaller Chinese community seems to be following a similar pattern since bilingual services were established in 1975.

The D.C. Setting

The D.C. bilingual program serves a relatively small population in comparison with other large urban school districts, providing direct instructional services or counseling for approximately 1500 students who speak languages other than English and 500 English-speaking students in eleven elementary and three secondary schools. The program has thus served as a manageably researchable miniature which can be compared with the experience of others. It is hoped that the detail described will yield insights for others implementing bilingual education programs around the country. No one bilingual program can provide others with an exportable model, because the social and linguistic context of each school system that has students with limited English proficiency is unique. Therefore, this study is not meant to serve as a prototype for other bilingual programs but rather as a guide to the complexity of evolution of this innovation, along with the hope that it provide for a different kind of school environment for both students with limited English proficiency and for English speakers.

One characteristic unique to Washington, D.C. is that the minority Hispanic community (estimated to be roughly 5-10 percent) exists within a Black majority (73 percent), with Blacks dominating local politics and school administration. The give-and-take at the central administrative level in local school politics is therefore largely negotiated with a minority group already somewhat sensitive to the need for different school structures for the variety of school children being served.

Another feature is the great heterogeneity of the linguistic groups being served by the bilingual program. For the last fifteen to twenty years, the Washington, D.C. area has played host to an increasing number of immigrants from many different parts of the world. Within the D.C. public schools, the largest group of international students is Spanish speakers (1,053 in 1979), but this group is very heterogeneous, with no single dominant group. Central Americans are a slight majority when the six countries are counted as one unit, but those who dominate the Hispanic community power structure are of middle-class background and come from a variety of Latin American countries. Likewise, the second largest linguistic group in the public schools, the Chinese, is greatly varied in background, with 279 students (in 1979) who speak seven different Chinese dialects and come from many different parts of China, Taiwan, and Hong Kong (Bilingual Office, 1979). Because of the heterogeneity of students to be served and the fact that they are scattered throughout the schools of the District, the D.C. bilingual program has a variety of models being implemented in each school, ranging from two-way maintenance bilingual education, to transitional bilingual classes, to English as a second language (ESL) classes with some content area instruction in the native language, and including Spanish as a second language (SSL) instruction for English-speaking students in schools organized around a cluster concept. Therefore, this study discusses a variety of models of implementation of bilingual education within a very heterogeneous school setting.

QUALITATIVE RESEARCH

With this type of study, there can be no true beginning, middle, or end. No problems are solved (Diesing, 1971). For the researcher, each new insight uncovered new areas that raised additional questions and concerns. In trying to be as comprehensive as possible in a study of this nature, one must check and cross-check data through community and school office files, through interviews with many people at many different levels, and through participation in day-to-day activities in the schools and community. This process of soaking in the total environment is endless. Therefore, the analysis does not present tidy answers; rather, it tries to describe the many layers of reality that are a part of everyday school life. No one can say that the Washington, D.C. bilingual program has solved all problems for students who speak other languages. There are many questions left unanswered, and many unresolved tensions, unaccomplished goals, and new concerns. Yet some changes have taken place in both the community and the schools that seem to be significant in various ways for many of the people involved. This case study tries to show the constructive nature of that complexity.

IMPLICATIONS OF THE STUDY

The case study description has significant messages for bilingual program administrators, bilingual school personnel, program evaluators, parents, and community members. It extends the change literature through focus on the priorities of local planners as central to the successful evolution of a project, rather than evaluation based on implementation of an original federal or centralist blueprint. It provides detailed description of the complexities of a school innovation, demonstrating the need for school personnel to be open to constant adaptation to changing priorities matched with the unpredictable realities of school politics. It illustrates the creative use of many aspects of what are termed unresolved tensions in working toward constructive change.

REFERENCES

Diesing, Paul. *Patterns of Discovery in the Social Sciences.* Chicago: Aldine-Atherton, 1971.

District of Columbia, Board of Education, Bilingual Office. *A Linguistic and Cultural Profile of the Student Population of the District of Columbia Public School System.* Washington, D.C.: Board of Education, Bilingual Office, 1979.

Dulay, Heidi, and Burt, Marina. *Why Bilingual Education? A Summary of Research Findings.* Poster. San Francisco: Bloomsbury West Lau General Assistance Center, 1976.

Farrar, Eleanor; DeSanctis, John E.; and Cohen, David K. *Views from Below: Implementation Research in Education.* Cambridge, Mass.: Huron Institute, 1979.

Fishman, Joshua A. *Language Loyalty in the United States: The Maintenance and Perception of Non-English Mother Tongues by American Ethnic and Religious Groups.* The Hague: Mouton, 1966.

_____ . *Bilingual Education: An International Sociological Perspective.* Rowley, Mass.: Newbury House, 1976.

Hargreaves, David H. *Social Relations in a Secondary School.* London: Routledge and Kegan Paul, 1967.

Kleinfeld, Judith Smilg. *Eskimo School on the Andreafsky: A Study of Effective Bicultural Education.* New York: Praeger, 1979.

Levy, Gerald E. *Ghetto School.* Indianapolis: Bobbs-Merrill, 1970.

Marsh, David; Cassidy, Sheila; and Mora, Linda. "The Need for Enthnographic Evaluation in Bilingual-Bicultural Education." Paper presented at the California Association of Program Evaluators' Conference, March 1980, Los Angeles.

Modiano, Nancy. *Indian Education in the Chiapas Highlands.* New York: Holt, Rinehart and Winston, 1973.

Ogbu, John U. *The Next Generation: An Ethnography of Education in an Urban Neighborhood.* New York: Academic Press, 1974.

Peshkin, Alan. *Growing Up American: Schooling and Survival of Community.* Chicago: University of Chicago Press, 1978.

Philips, Susan U. "Acquisition of Rules for Appropriate Speech Usage." In *Bilingualism and Language Contact: Georgetown University Round Table on Languages and Linguistics 1970,* edited by James E. Alatis. Washington, D.C.: Georgetown University Press, 1970.

Rand Corporation. *Federal Programs Supporting Educational Change.* Rand Change Agent Study, vols. I-VII. Santa Monica, Calif.: Rand Corporation, 1974-77.

Read, John; Spolsky, Bernard; and Neundorf, Alice. "Socioeconomic Implications of Bilingual Education on the Navajo Reservation." In *The Bilingual Child,* edited by António Simões. New York: Academic Press, 1976.

Rosenfeld, Gerry. *Shut Those Thick Lips! A Study of Slum School Failure.* New York: Holt, Rinehart and Winston, 1971.

Spindler, George D., ed. *Education and Cultural Process: Toward an Anthropology of Education.* New York: Holt, Rinehart and Winston, 1974.

Spolsky, Bernard. "Bilingual Education in the United States." In *Georgetown University Round Table on Languages and Linguistics 1978: International Dimensions of Bilingual Education,* edited by James E. Alatis. Washington, D.C.: Georgetown University Press, 1978.

Swain, Merrill. "Bilingual Education: Research and Its Implications." In *On TESOL '79.* Washington, D.C.: Teachers of English to Speakers of Other Languages, 1979.

Troike, Rudolph. "Research Evidence for the Effectiveness of Bilingual Education." *National Association for Bilingual Education Journal* 3 (1978): 13-24.

Tucker, G. Richard. *Implications for U.S. Bilingual Education: Evidence from Canadian Research.* Focus, no. 2. Rosslyn, Va.: National Clearinghouse for Bilingual Education, 1980.

Wolcott, Harry F. *The Man in the Principal's Office: An Ethnography.* New York: Holt, Rinehart and Winston, 1973.

_____ . *Teachers vs. Technocrats: An Educational Innovation in Anthropological Perspective.* Eugene, Oreg.: University of Oregon, Center for Educational Policy and Management, 1977.

A Comparison of Bilingual Oral Language Reading Skills among Limited-English-Speaking Children from Spanish-Speaking Backgrounds

Vicki Gunther

Semifinalist, Outstanding Dissertations
National Advisory Council on Bilingual Education

Degree conferred August 1981
Northwestern University
Evanston, Illinois

Dissertation Committee:
Norman D. Bowers, *Chair*
Rae Moses
Arthur Smith

About the Author

Dr. Vicki Gunther is a Bilingual Coordinator in the Department of Multi-lingual Education of the Chicago Public Schools. She has also served as a Bilingual Resource Teacher and an ESL specialist in the Chicago schools. Her publications have been in the area of approaches to teaching reading to limited English-proficient students.

SUMMARY

This dissertation was designed to provide practitioners with data upon which to base instructional decisions in the area of bilingual education. Oral language and reading skills were studied to determine whether there were significant differences among limited-English-speaking students grouped according to type of reading approach. Additionally, the study focused on identifying sociological, instructional, and linguistic variables associated with the acquisition of skills.

The sample consisted of 306 Spanish-background students of limited English proficiency, ages six, eight, and ten who were pre- and posttested in 1977–78 on seven oral language and reading measures in Spanish and English.

Findings indicated that for some skill areas, bilingual program participants performed on a comparable basis with non-bilingual program participants. For other skill areas, non-bilingual program participants performed better. These findings should be interpreted with caution since the cumulative benefits of bilingual instruction do not always surface in cross-sectional designs.

PURPOSE OF THE STUDY

Educators generally agree that the entire school curriculum is based upon a student's ability to read. Numerous studies have indicated that the level of reading ability is a reliable predictor of academic success in subject areas of instruction. With regard to students of limited English proficiency, it is apparent that their ability to read in English is related to their ability to speak and understand English. Through specialized programs of instruction, school systems across the country are trying to meet the needs of these students. Among these programs, bilingual education is the most prevalent.

One of the principal goals of this dissertation was to study the effects of teaching reading, under different linguistic conditions, on the acquisition of oral language and reading skills among groups of limited-English-speaking students. The different linguistic conditions included: (1) teaching reading in the native language prior to the formal introduction of English reading; (2) teaching reading in the native language and English concurrently; and (3) teaching reading in English exclusively. Another goal was to identify sociological, linguistic, and instructional variables that appear to relate to the acquisition of skills.

BACKGROUND

Nationwide, there are more than five million school-age children who speak a language other than English or live in households in which a language other than English is spoken (*FORUM*, 1978). The need to design effective educational programs for these children is one of the most pressing tasks confronting policymakers and educators at federal, state, and local levels.

However, basic program designs and subsequent modifications require quality research and evaluation. As stated by Troike (1978):

> Bilingual education is in critical need of research, both basic and operational, and unless it receives this support, this great experiment could become just another passing effort in the history of American education which failed to achieve its goals—to the detriment of millions of school children and of our whole society. (p. 2)

The need for more systematic research on the effects of bilingual education is especially important in light of the proliferation of programs throughout the country. A review of the status of research on bilingual education indicated that there is not yet a systematic data base upon which to form generalizations (Troike, 1978). However, research priorities recently have been identified and include studying the effects of different reading instructional approaches and problems of transfer from native language reading to reading in a second language.

The majority of studies have focused on the different ways the first and second languages are sequenced in the bilingual education curriculum. Alternatives include the native language approach where children are taught to read first in their native language (Modiano, 1968; Rosier, 1977); the concurrent approach where children are taught to read in two languages concurrently (Cohen, 1975); and the immersion approach where children learn to read first in the second language (Lambert and Tucker, 1972). As of this date, there is little conclusive evidence that one approach is inherently superior in terms of successful acquisition of oral language and reading skills (Cohen and Laosa, 1976).

In an attempt to reconcile the apparently contradictory findings, Cummins (1976; 1979) proposed two hypotheses: the threshold hypothesis and the developmental interdependence hypothesis. According to the former, Cummins theorized that there may be threshold levels of linguistic competence children must attain in order to avoid cognitive deficits. The developmental interdependence hypothesis relates to the functional interdependence between first and second language skills.

Bilingual education programs differ on a number of levels and for this reason it has been difficult to construct comprehensive research designs to assess program effectiveness. Both proponents and opponents have been able to support their arguments by citing available studies which either support or negate the effectiveness of bilingual education. This has contributed to the present state of confusion among practitioners.

To design and implement effective programs, the practitioner is in dire need of answers to basic questions. What are the basic competencies that teachers should demonstrate in a bilingual program? Are particular organizational models more effective than others? Should all limited English speakers first learn to read in their native language? When should English be introduced? When should students exit from a bilingual program? What are the best ways of teaching reading? These questions could be continued ad infinitum, and some questions are yet to be formulated.

STATEMENT OF THE PROBLEM

While all of the above questions are of practical interest to the educator, the teaching of reading to limited English speakers and the acquisition of related skills were selected as the focus for this study.

Based on ten years of experience working within one of the largest school systems in the nation, the author often found more than one bilingual reading approach being practiced in various classrooms of a given school. For purposes here, the term *approach* is used to refer to the different ways of sequencing language in teaching reading. Selection of the language or languages for initial reading instruction was often at the discretion of the local administrator or classroom teacher.

As a result of the author's observations, several questions were raised. Were there specific criteria used by school personnel in selecting a bilingual reading approach? Were specific student characteristics considered, or was selection based on staff characteristics and physical facilities? Were school administrators aware that there *were* choices available? Again, the choices were many, including what text to use, maximum time to be devoted to reading, and skill-area emphasis. In short, there did not appear to be any systematic manner of selecting the language medium of instruction or the other variables mentioned.

The present study was designed to investigate and compare student performance in (1) the acquisition of oral language skills in English and (2) the acquisition of reading skills in English and Spanish.

The first problem investigated in this study was whether there were significant differences in the acquisition of oral language and reading skills among groups of limited-English-speaking children, ages six, eight, and ten, receiving instruction through different bilingual reading approaches. For purposes of this study, three bilingual reading approaches have been defined:

- *Native Language Approach (NL):* Initial reading instruction is given, on a daily basis, in the native language (L_1), e.g., Spanish, prior to formal instruction in English (L_2) reading. When students master basic reading skills in L_1 and oral skills in L_2, reading instruction is presented in L_2.

- *Concurrent Approach (CON):* Initial reading instruction is given in both L_1 and L_2 on a daily basis.

- *Direct Method (DM):* Reading instruction is given exclusively in L_2 on a daily basis.

The second problem was to determine other sociological, linguistic, and instructional variables which appeared to relate to the acquisition of skills among limited English speakers, ages six, eight and ten. Sociological variables included sex, ethnic background, and socioeconomic level. Linguistics variables included oral fluency levels in English and Spanish. Instructional variables included enrollment in a bilingual education program, years enrolled in the program, instruction in English as a second language

(ESL), teacher training, and teacher attitudes toward second language learners.

METHODOLOGY

Hypotheses

Two major hypotheses were derived:

Hypothesis 1. There were no differences among limited-English-speaking students, ages six, eight, and ten, in different reading instructional groups on measures of oral English skills, and reading skills in English and Spanish.

Hypothesis 2. There were no relationships among independent variables and dependent variables measuring oral language and reading skills for groups of limited-English-speaking students, ages six, eight, and ten.

Both hypotheses were further subdivided for each of the three age groups by skill area, i.e., oral English, English reading, and Spanish reading.

Design

The subjects were Spanish background students, ages six, eight, and ten, who were limited in English and enrolled in thirteen public and nonpublic elementary schools in the Chicago metropolitan area. Of the 379 students pretested, 306 were available for posttesting. Subjects were grouped according to three different reading approaches: the native language approach (NL), the concurrent approach (CON), and the direct method (DM).

For purposes here, the native language and concurrent approaches were considered as experimental, with the direct method being the control.

Table 1
Design

Age Group	Reading Instructional Group[a]	N	Total
6	NL	49	
	CON	39	
	DM	44	132
8	CON	62	
	DM	35	97
10	CON	51	
	DM	26	77

[a] NL = Native Language Approach; CON = Concurrent Approach; DM = Direct Method.

Selection of Sample

Subjects were selected from more than one classroom and more than one school for each cell. By obtaining a cross-section of students throughout the city, the following objectives could be accomplished:

- The generalizability of results would not be limited to only a few schools with similar characteristics.

- The treatment effects on groups of students from more than one ethnic background could be investigated.

- The treatment effects on students of varying socioeconomic levels could be considered.

- Individual teacher effects would be minimized.

Experimental groups were selected from schools implementing bilingual programs for a minimum of three years to ensure that the programs would be operating, for the most part, within guidelines, that teachers would have received inservice training on program objectives and goals, and that sufficient bilingual instructional materials would be available.

Schools with Spanish language programs were selected because they were able to meet the above criteria. Additionally, more testing instruments were available in Spanish.

The most crucial decision was made with reference to the control group, which consisted of students receiving reading instruction in English only. Inasmuch as Article 14C of the Illinois School Code mandates bilingual instruction in all public schools with twenty or more children with limited English-speaking fluency who share a common home language, there were two alternatives in terms of finding a control group: (1) select public schools with an enrollment of fewer than twenty students of the same minority language group, or (2) select nonpublic schools adjacent to the public schools. For many reasons (which are cited in the dissertation), the second alternative was chosen.

Teachers in eight public and five nonpublic schools were requested to provide lists of Spanish-background students in their classrooms whom they judged to be of limited English-speaking fluency (operationally defined according to the *Functional Language Survey*). Teachers were also requested to provide information on age and ethnic background.

A simple random-selection approach was employed in which every other name was chosen. The lists were then reviewed so that equal numbers of students at varying proficiency levels were selected. With class lists including students from more than one ethnic background, efforts were made to ensure selection of equal numbers of students from Puerto Rican and Mexican backgrounds.

Data Collection

Two types of data were collected: data relating to students and data relating to teachers. Student data included background information on the following: sex, birthdate, birthplace, birthplace of mother and father, ethnic background, approximate number of years in the United States (mainland), years in a U.S. school, enrollment in a bilingual program, participation in a free lunch program, welfare, and information on language(s) used in reading instruction, minutes per day, and when instruction began. The following test instruments were used: *Functional Language Survey (FLS), Language Assessment Scales (LAS)*—English and Spanish versions, the *Stanford Early School Achievement Test (SESAT)* for six year olds only, the *Stanford Diagnostic Reading Test (SDRT)* for eight and ten year olds, the *CRS Placement/Diagnostic Test (CRS)*— English and Spanish versions, and the *Prueba de Lectura (PRUEBA)*.

A questionnaire was developed to obtain background information on the teachers of students in the study. Additionally, data were collected on teacher attitudes toward second language learners.

DATA ANALYSIS

Preliminary analysis of the data revealed that instructional reading groups were not equivalent on all pretreatment variables. For this reason, multivariate and univariate analyses of covariance techniques were used to determine if there were statistically significant differences among reading instructional groups.

Regression analysis was selected as the statistical technique to determine the degree to which selected independent variables related to the successful acquisition of skills.

Prior to using inferential statistical procedures on posttest data, a variety of descriptive statistical techniques were used on pretest and posttest data.

FINDINGS

Hypothesis 1

1. *Oral English:* For all three age samples, students receiving English reading instruction exclusively attained higher posttest mean scores on the LAS oral English measure, compared with the other reading groups. However, the results of one-way ANCOVA procedures were significant only for six year olds ($p < .01$) and eight year olds ($p < .05$). These results indicated that, among younger students, those receiving reading instruction exclusively in English performed better than students receiving bilingual instruction. For older students (ten year olds), it appeared that acquisition of oral skills in English was not affected by the type of instruction approach. The older students also made relatively smaller posttest gains in oral English as compared to the younger students. A similar finding was found in a study by Fathman (1976), who stated that younger students generally receive more oral language instruction than older students.

These results should be interpreted with caution since this was a cross-sectional design. Current research in bilingual education has emphasized that the cumulative benefits of bilingual instruction may not always surface in cross-sectional designs (Barik and Swain, 1974; Rosier and Farella, 1976). Furthermore, although several design controls were introduced in this study, some of the preliminary analyses revealed that the instructional groups were not initially equivalent. This might suggest that the English-only group of nonpublic school students was, in fact, not a representative sample from the same population as the public school students. It should also be noted that an analysis of the bilingual program participants' performance revealed that they *did* make posttest gains in oral English, with the native language group obtaining higher scores than the concurrent group.

2. *English Reading:* For six year olds, the results of the statistical procedures indicated significant differences among the three reading instructional groups. Follow-up procedures indicated that both of the dependent reading variables contributed to the significant multivariate effect. The bilingual program participants who received reading instruction in two languages performed better in English reading than the other two groups. This substantiates current studies (Troike, 1978), which have shown that a bilingual instructional approach may facilitate learning to read in English.

With reference to students who had received reading instruction in Spanish during the first seven months of the school year, gains were also made on English posttest measures even though they had not been exposed to the same amount of English reading instruction as the other two groups. This could suggest transfer of skills from Spanish to English.

Multivariate analyses of covariance were not significant for either the eight or ten year olds, suggesting that participation in a bilingual program had no adverse effects on the acquisition of reading skills. Additional benefits resulting from participation in a bilingual program can only be determined by further testing of students in the specific subject areas by evaluating student progress longitudinally.

3. *Spanish Reading:* The MANCOVAs indicated significant differences for all three age samples. An analysis of posttest mean scores indicated that in all cases, the bilingual program participants performed better on tests of Spanish reading than students who did not receive any reading instruction in Spanish. This was to be expected.

Hypothesis 2

Results from the regression techniques, used to test the second hypothesis relating to independent variables associated with the acquisition of oral language and reading skills, can be summarized as follows:

1. Among young children, L_1 fluency was a good predictor of L_2 oral skills.

2. For all age groups, L_1 oral skills were consistent predictors of L_1 reading skills.

3. For younger children, ESL instruction, teacher training, and teacher attitudes were positively associated with the acquisition of skills.

4. No definitive trends were observed with respect to other variables such as sex, ethnic background, and socioeconomic status.

IMPLICATIONS AND CONCLUSIONS

Based on the findings of this study, it remains difficult to make one general statement regarding the superiority of a particular bilingual reading approach. A simple answer to selection of a reading approach may not even exist. Perhaps a more complex solution can be found with reference to student characteristics interacting with approach. For example, the concurrent or immersion approach may be more appropriate for students whose motivation is high and who have developed competence in their first language (Cummins, 1979). For others, whose motivation is low and who have not developed competence in the first language, the native language approach may be more appropriate.

Current research suggests that a thorough knowledge of L_2 is a prerequisite to the development of reading skills in L_2. If this is the case, it would appear wise to delay L_2 reading instruction until the student has attained oral competence in L_2. Results from this study suggest that younger children exposed to initial reading instruction in the native language, as opposed to both languages concurrently, are more successful in acquiring oral L_2 skills. This suggests that young children might be more apt to acquire L_2 oral skills if they do not receive reading instruction in the two languages concurrently. The introduction of initial reading skills in the native language prior to the second language might also foster the development of those higher cognitive skills needed in proficient reading.

Because there is very little research available in this area, a program planner must be careful not to select arbitrarily one reading approach for all limited-English-speaking students. Perhaps for some linguistic groups, an immersion or concurrent approach should be considered and for others, a native language approach where reading instruction in L_2 is delayed.

Also to be considered are parental expectations in the area of bilingual education. Variation in parental aspirations is bound to have an effect on student performance and should be seriously considered as one of the factors in program planning.

Program administrators should give consideration to the expansion of bilingual education programs for preschool and kindergarten children—programs that should generally emphasize oral language development. Based on the results of this study, the findings suggest that perhaps less instructional time should be spent on native language arts instruction for older children.

Findings of this study also suggest that ESL instruction does make a difference, especially for younger children. School administrators should continue to train bilingual and monolingual staff in ESL methodology through continuing staff development and inservice education programs.

Although this study did not deal with program evaluation, it appears that it would be the next logical step for consideration in overall program planning and refinement. If this is the case, more observational techniques should be used so that actual teaching techniques and interactions among teachers and students can be analyzed qualitatively and quantitatively.

Additionally, research designs should be selected that promote investigations of salient student and teacher characteristics interacting with a variety of educational treatments.

In conclusion, the number of issues discussed clearly indicates a need for additional research on the teaching and acquisition of oral language and reading skills among second language learners. Recommendations for future research include: studies to assess longitudinally particular educational approaches; studies focusing on affective variables; psycholinguistic-oriented research, including transfer; studies focusing on the relationship between L_1 and L_2, including identification of minimum levels of competence; and finally, studies identifying specific teaching techniques that contribute to the academic success of second language learners in all areas of the curriculum.

REFERENCES

Barik, H.C., and Swain, M. "English-French Bilingual Education in the Early Grades: The Elgin Study." *Modern Language Journal* 58, no. 8 (1974): 392-403.

Cohen, A.D. *A Sociolinguistic Approach to Bilingual Education: Experiments in the American Southwest.* Rowley, Mass.: Newbury House, 1975.

‗‗‗‗‗‗ , and Laosa, L. "Second Language Instruction: Some Research Considerations." *Journal of Curriculum Studies* 8 (1976): 149-65.

Cummins, J. *The Influence of Bilingualism on Cognitive Growth: A Synthesis of Research Findings and Explanatory Hypotheses.* Working Papers on Bilingualism, no. 9. Toronto: Ontario Institute for Studies in Education, 1976. (ERIC ED 125-311.)

‗‗‗‗‗‗ . "Linguistic Interdependence and the Educational Development of Bilingual Children." *Review of Educational Research* 49, no. 2 (1979): 222-51.

Fathman, A.K. "Variables Affecting the Successful Learning of English as a Second Language." *TESOL Quarterly* 10, no. 4 (1976): 433-41.

Functional Language Survey. Chicago, Ill.: Board of Education of the City of Chicago, 1977.

Lambert, W.E., and Tucker, G.E. *Bilingual Education of Children: The St. Lambert Experiment.* Rowley, Mass.: Newbury House, 1972.

Modiano, N. "National or Mother Language in Beginning Reading: A Comparative Study." *Research in the Teaching of English* 1 (1968): 32-48.

"NCES Releases Statistical Findings on Language Minorities in the U.S." National Clearinghouse for Bilingual Education *FORUM* 1, no. 8 (October 1978): 4-5.

Rosier, P.W. "A Comparative Study of Two Approaches of Introducing Initial Reading to Navajo Children: The Direct Method and the Native Language Method." (Ph.D. dissertation, Northern Arizona University, 1977.) *Dissertation Abstracts International* 38 (1977): 1167A. (Ann Arbor, Mich.: University Microfilms No. 77-18, 788.)

‗‗‗‗‗‗ , and Farella, M. "Bilingual Education at Rock Point—Some Early Results." *TESOL Quarterly* 10, no. 4 (1976): 379-88.

Troike, R. *Research Priorities in Bilingual Education.* Arlington, Va.: Center for Applied Linguistics, 1974.

‗‗‗‗‗‗ . *Research Evidence for the Effectiveness of Bilingual Education.* Rosslyn, Va.: National Clearinghouse for Bilingual Education, 1978.

Effectiveness of Individualized Bilingual Instruction for Migrant Students

Beverly B. McConnell

Semifinalist, Outstanding Dissertations
National Advisory Council on Bilingual Education

Degree conferred June 1980
Washington State University
Pullman, Washington

Dissertation Committee:
William P. McDougall, *Chair*
Toshio Akamine
Thomas A. Brigham

About the Author

Dr. Beverly B. McConnell is the Evaluator for IBI, a Title VII demonstration program operating in Texas and Washington State, which is funded through the Pasco School District, Pasco, Washington. She was Research Director for Metcor and a consultant on migrant programs in the Office of Child Development, both in Washington, D.C. She has published articles on bilingual education and migrant day care centers.

SUMMARY

The purpose of the study was to see if bilingual education (use of two languages as a medium of instruction) is significantly more effective than traditional education for Spanish-speaking children in teaching them both languages and academic subjects, and whether longer periods of attendance in the bilingual program increase its effectiveness.

The major finding was that children in the bilingual program made significantly superior progress in both language acquisition and academic subjects after even short-term attendance in the bilingual program, and each added period of attendance increased their superior achievement over the scores received by children not attending the bilingual program.

These findings were replicated for several cohorts of children over a six-year period. Similar findings were found within every age group, for both sexes, for children who started the program with different levels of bilingual skills, for children representing different levels of ability, and finally for children served in communities reinforcing first language maintenance as well as those in communities pressuring toward transition to English.

STATEMENT OF THE PROBLEM

Around the world linguistic minorities have a record of doing very poorly in school. The Mexican American child in the United States has a history of failure in the schools that is by now well documented (U.S. Commission on Civil Rights, 1971).

The past decade has seen a growing number of educational programs developed in which basic instruction is provided in the mother tongue as well as English. They are based on the premise that bilingual instruction will enable children to improve their academic skills while they are acquiring linguistic competence in two languages. Most of these programs provide bilingual instruction over a period of years; yet there have been few studies that have looked at program effects resulting from bilingual instruction in terms of the length of time the child has attended the program. This study has developed a longitudinal design incorporating tests from a six-year period. This allows the examination of the effects of bilingual instruction for several cohorts of children after different periods of attendance ranging from less than a year up to exposure for three or more years.

PURPOSE OF THE STUDY

The purpose of the study was to address the general question: How does the length of attendance in a bilingual program, in which the child's primary language is used as one of the languages of instruction, affect the proficiency of Spanish-speaking children in both English and Spanish, and in the academic subjects of math and reading?

89

THEORETICAL FRAMEWORK

One explanation given for the record of school failure among linguistic minorities is the theory that if children are not given the opportunity to develop their mother tongue through its use as a medium of instruction in school, not only their linguistic development in the mother tongue but also their learning of the official or national language will be hindered, with predictable effects on their achievement in all language-related academic subjects. The term given this condition is *double semilingualism,* meaning the incomplete learning of two languages (Skutnabb-Kangas, 1979).

There is support for this theory from a number of research studies coming from Sweden. Toukomaa (reported in Skutnabb-Kangas, 1979) compared the linguistic development in Swedish of immigrant children from Finland, based on the age at which their linguistic development in Finnish had been cut off by their immigration. The preschoolers who had no opportunity for schooling in Finland in their primary language were the worst off in learning Swedish; children who had one or two years of schooling in Finland did better in learning Swedish after immigration; and children with three or more years of schooling in their native tongue before immigration showed the greatest ability to acquire Swedish as a second language.

A number of other studies offer a variety of explanations of why it should be important for children to be schooled in their mother tongue, and why the abandonment of one language as another is learned would have a detrimental effect. Collison (1974) found that children can reason at a higher conceptual level in their mother tongue than in a second language. Gunnel Wrede (1972, in Paulston, 1975) proposed that literacy in a language provides a richness of language development not possible through oral usage alone, and that literacy in a language is not likely unless there is some schooling in that language. Paulston (1975) suggested that if a minority family was attempting to switch usage to a second language they knew poorly, and used this exclusively around their children, that the children might grow up never hearing a fully developed language. This would deprive them of a cognitive basis for rules of linguistic usage and would hinder them in any language they attempted to learn.

Gudschinsky (1971) posed a number of sociocultural reasons why children should do better if their initial schooling involved their native tongue—such as lessening the cultural shock of starting school and building identity and self-esteem. Modiano (1973) suggested motivational factors through identification with native speakers.

Several scholars have examined the contradictory evidence from studies that show negative and positive effects associated with children's attempting to learn a second language and academic subjects through a second language. Gaarder (in Paulston, 1975) distinguished between "folk bilingualism" and "elitist bilingualism" as a key to different consequences of bilingualism or bilingual study. In folk bilingualism a second language is acquired involuntarily in order to survive since the second or national language controls access to jobs and social and political institutions, as well as acceptance by the dominant majority. On the other hand, there is bilingualism by choice, to which Gaarder refers as elitist bilingualism, in which members of the dominant language group, particularly those from the middle and upper classes, add a second language to their repertoire without this being accompanied by any academic retardation.

The difference in effect of these two types of bilingualism suggested by Lambert (1975) is found in the amount of support given the first language. In folk bilingualism the home language is often abandoned as the minority seeks to adopt the dominant tongue. In elitist bilingualism there is no danger of the second language replacing the first because the first language is a prestige language, usually the dominant or national language.

Cummins (1976, 1979) has pulled together the threads of reasoning in these various explanations and proposed what he calls the "threshold hypothesis." This hypothesis holds that there may be threshold levels of linguistic competence that bilingual children must attain in both their first and second languages in order to avoid cognitive deficits through study in the second language, and to allow the potentially beneficial aspects of becoming bilingual to influence their cognitive growth.

In addition to the theoretical basis supporting the need for dual language instruction, there is an empirical basis for predicting effects of such a program. The empirical studies are contradictory, suggesting that both child input and external factors relating to language policy and the relationships between linguistic groups may interact with educational programs, thus obscuring their interpretation as predictors in different sociolinguistic settings. The international studies in Canada (Lambert and Tucker, 1972) and the Philippines (Ramos, Aguilar, and Sibayan, 1967) provide mixed evidence as to the effectiveness of second language instruction and the most desirable sequence for inclusion of first language instruction. Several studies from the United States provide some longitudinal basis for predicting positive results from bilingual education using dual-medium instruction (Rosier and Farella, 1976; Barlow, 1976; Kyle, 1976; Leyba, 1978; and Cohen, 1975). Several survey studies offer general support for the premise that bilingual education has a positive effect (Paulston, 1975; Troike, 1978; and Zappert and Cruz, 1977). These studies also suggest many variables that might affect the outcome of bilingual education—such as age, bilingual status when entering the program, the interaction between ability and achievement, sex of participants, and the importance of community attitudes toward language shift and language maintenance—all of which were incorporated into the research questions posed for this study as outlined in the following section.

MAIN HYPOTHESES/RESEARCH QUESTIONS

This study posed the following research questions:

1. Does participation in a program of bilingual instruction improve children's proficiency in English?

2. Does participation in a program of bilingual instruction improve children's proficiency in Spanish?

3. Does participation in a program of bilingual instruction lead to improvement in skills in English reading?

4. Does participation in a program of bilingual instruction lead to improvement in skills in math?

5. How is the effect of participation in a program of bilingual instruction affected by comparative levels of ability?

6. How does the effect of participation in a program of bilingual instruction differ by age level?

7. How does the effect of participation in a program of bilingual instruction differ according to sex?

8. How does the effect of participation in a program of bilingual instruction differ based on the extent to which children are bilingual when they enter the program?

9. How does the effect of participation in a program of bilingual instruction differ based on whether the program is operating in a community that encourages language shift or one that reinforces maintenance of the non-English language?

To guide the analysis of data these research questions were translated into null hypotheses that identified the tests to be used and means of grouping test data on the independent variables.

STUDY DESIGN

Throughout this study *bilingual instruction* is used to mean an educational program in which two languages are used as the medium of instruction to teach both languages and academic subjects.

The sample for this study was drawn from children enrolled in a demonstration bilingual program for children of migrant farm workers. Some of these children were enrolled in a "home base" community on the south Texas border, and some were enrolled in parallel programs in Washington State in an area where many Texas-based migrants come to work. The name of the program is IBI, standing for "Individualized Bilingual Instruction." It uses an individualized bilingual curriculum in Spanish and English that offers sequential instruction in oral language, reading, and math from preschool through third grade.

The sample for the study was limited to children whose primary language was Spanish. Since the analysis planned required the use of standard scores, and for two of the tests standard scores were only available for children age five and over, this further limited the sample to children over the age of five. Beyond these two limitations, the study sample included all children in the IBI program or comparison group who received all four tests (Spanish vocabulary, English vocabulary, math, and English reading) during the years 1974–79. This resulted in a study sample of 1,020 sets of tests.

In order to judge how children would have progressed academically without benefit of individualized bilingual instruction, a "no treatment" group was required. To achieve this, the pretest scores of all children entering the program during the six-year period went into a data bank to make up a baseline of test scores before benefit of the bilingual program. Since the program enrolled more children at the younger ages, the baseline of pretest scores from the upper age levels were slower to accumulate. To augment the no-treatment group at these age levels, therefore, some migrant children who met the same criteria as used for the admission of children to the program under study were tested in a neighboring school. This combination of scores is referred to as the baseline-comparison group, and is shown on tables as the *0 Attendance* group.

Attendance in the bilingual program was kept cumulatively for each individual child, and posttests were given after each 100-day interval of program attendance. For analysis purposes these tests were assigned to five attendance categories based on the usual 180-day school year: *0 Attendance, 1/2 Year, 1 Year, 2 Years,* and *3 Years.* Each test was assigned to the category closest to the child's cumulative attendance at the time of testing.

A t-test was used to analyze the significance of differences between means when there were only two groups being compared; one- and two-way analysis of variance was used for significance of differences involving more than two groups. Both procedures used the SPSS (Nie, 1970, 1975) computer package.

FINDINGS, CONCLUSIONS, AND IMPLICATIONS

Findings Regarding Language Proficiency Related to Length of Attendance in Bilingual Program

The analysis of test scores from the six-year period showed that the mean vocabulary scores of children in both Spanish and English increased with each added period of attendance in the bilingual program. The increase of scores resulted in differences between groups based on length of attendance in the bilingual program that was statistically significant beyond the 0.01 level. The progressive gains with longer attendance were also clearly "educationally significant" in that children in the baseline comparison group demonstrated very low scores in English in reference to their Spanish scores, and children who had attended the bilingual program for three years had brought their English vocabularly scores up almost equal to their scores in Spanish, which was their primary language, and in this time their Spanish had improved as well.

Macnamara (1966) postulated that there is a "balance effect" involved in the learning of two languages, and that a child acquiring a second language does so at the expense of lowered proficiency in the first language. Clearly the findings from this study contradict this hypothesis in that gains in the second language have been made without adverse effects on the primary language.

Previous studies have had mixed results as to whether acquisition of a second language can be achieved without a loss in the first language. Lambert (1975) analyzed contradictory studies and hypothesized that there were situations that would produce what he termed *additive bilingualism,* meaning adding a second language at no expense to the first, and *subtractive bilingualism,* when language shift occurred and children lost the primary language as they learned the second. Additive bilingualism occurred in most cases, he observed, when the primary language was reinforced because (1) it was the dominant language of the community, or (2) the children came from middle- or upper-class homes providing much home support for good language development in the primary language. Subtractive bilingualism occurred when the primary language was a minority language or children came from a poverty-level home that did not provide support for good language development.

This study is therefore important in that it examines children from a minority language group and a poverty background in which the home environment does not support good language development. Nonetheless, their growing bilingualism has been "additive." It may be concluded from these data that when Spanish is supported through a bilingual program, minority children may gain added skills in English at no cost to their Spanish competence, which may significantly improve as well.

Findings Regarding Math and English Reading Related to Length of Attendance in the Bilingual Program

Scores of children in the no-treatment, baseline-comparison group indicated that without the bilingual program the average score of children in both math and English reading was more than one standard deviation below the norm based on standardized testing. The average English reading scores were in the range equivalent to the lowest 10 percent of children with whom this test was normed. Each period of attendance in the bilingual program brought about an increase in the average scores, with the mean reading score of children who had attended the bilingual program three years exactly at the national norm or fiftieth percentile.

In math the no treatment group had scores equivalent to the lowest 14 percent of children in the national norm group. With the bilingual program, scores rose rapidly with every added period of attendance so that the average score of children reached the national norm in two years, and children who had been in the bilingual program for three years had average math scores at the seventieth percentile, far above national norms.

These differences in scores based on program attendance were both educationally and statistically significant (0.01 level).

To test the stability of the effectiveness of the program, separate analyses were done for tests from the years 1974–75, 1976–77, and 1978–79. For each of these two-year periods, the pattern of findings was the same. Longer attendance in the bilingual program resulted in higher test scores, with the differences statistically significant at the 0.01 level.

The importance of finding that the pattern of gains was repeated for several cohorts of children over a six-year period is that it tends to rule out other possible causes for the improved academic skills of children. A "Hawthorne effect," i.e., a positive program effect due merely to the attention that participants receive, is a frequently cited alternative explanation for children's educational gains in an experimental situation. However, it is unlikely that a Hawthorne effect could be sustained over a six-year period. Several different groups of children and a turnover of teachers were involved in the repeated replications. This randomizes child ability factors and teacher effects, giving added confidence that the positive effect of attendance on increasing academic skills represents a stable effect of the bilingual program.

Engle (1975) reviewed twenty-five studies of bilingual education and made repeated reference to the finding that initially children enrolled in a bilingual program had lower scores than their monolingually schooled counterparts, and that it took about four years for them to "catch up." In this study there was no period in which the bilingually schooled children fell behind. The superior achievement of children attending the bilingual program over the no-treatment group after just a half school year was already statistically significant at the 0.01 level, and each added period of attendance widened the difference.

Findings Related to Comparative Levels of Ability within the Sample

Children were divided into low-, medium-, or high-ability groups according to their relative placement within this sample of children on their initial Spanish vocabulary score when enrolling in the IBI program. Separate analyses measuring effects of length of attendance in the bilingual program were made for each ability group. The findings were that the program appears to be about equally effective with children whose ability would be considered low, medium, or high in math, reading, and learning English. However, it was more effective in raising Spanish vocabulary scores for the low-ability group. In the other subjects the primary difference in program effect was in the maximum score level reached, and the length of time it took for children to reach comparable scores.

Cummins (1979) observed that almost no research was available in the United States on differential effects based on ability, despite a very hetero-geneous population served in bilingual programs. Malherbe (1946) did a massive study in South Africa which reported that bilingually schooled children did better than students receiving schooling in either Afrikaans or English alone, and that this was especially true for the lower-intelligence group. The present study lends some support to Malherbe's finding.

Findings Related to Age Differences

At every age level, five through nine, there was a strong positive correlation between test scores and longer periods of program attendance that applied to both English and Spanish vocabulary tests, and to math and English reading. The differences in scores between attendance groups was statistically significant beyond the 0.01 level only at age five for Spanish vocabulary, for all age levels in English vocabulary and math, and for all ages except age nine in English reading.

Findings Related to Sex Differences

Both boys and girls showed nearly parallel patterns of gains relating to their length of attendance in the bilingual program, and the differences related to period of attendance tended to far overshadow any differences that appeared related to sex. The statistical analysis showed that dividing the sample by sex produced no significant differences for test scores in English vocabulary or in math. However, boys were found to have higher scores in Spanish vocabulary overall, and the girls were found to have scores higher in English reading, and for these two subjects the differences were statistically significant at the 0.01 level.

Findings Relating to the Degree to Which Children were Bilingual When Entering the Program

Children were classified as monolingual, partial bilingual, or balanced bilin-gual based on relative scores in Spanish and English vocabulary on their pretests at the time of program entry. The effects of different periods of attendance in the bilingual program were then analyzed to see if the degree of initial bilingualism made participation in the bilingual program more or less beneficial for any of the groups.

On entry into the program, on all four tests, the children classified as monolingual had the lowest scores. Those classified as partial bilingual averaged somewhat higher scores. And those classified as balanced bilingual had the highest scores. This was true for English vocabulary and English reading, in which the test was given in English. However, it was also true for Spanish vocabulary and math tests, which were given in Spanish. Since all of the children had Spanish as their primary language, the degree of bilin-gualism depended on how much English they knew. Their scores on tests given in Spanish should presumably have been independent of the degree of bilingualism; nonetheless the finding was that increased bilingualism was associated with higher scores on all tests including those given in Spanish.

For all groups, longer periods of attendance in the bilingual program resulted in higher scores, with the difference between the groups becoming less the longer the period of attendance. In both math and reading, all three groups tended to reach national norms by three years of attendance in the bilingual program. Since the monolingual group of children started with the lowest scores, their gain was proportionately the largest and therefore there was found to be a significant interaction between bilingual classification and attendance for three of the four tests: math, English vocabulary, and Spanish vocabulary. The interaction effect was found to be not statistically significant for English reading. This appeared to be because all three groups were initially so low in English reading skills that there was less difference between them than for the other subjects, and the relative gains were therefore approximately the same. All three groups reached the national norm after three years' attendance in the bilingual program.

There have been a number of studies related to whether bilingualism is an "advantage" or "disadvantage." The early studies (Darcy, 1953, 1963) in most cases found that monolingual children had a superiority over bilinguals. These studies were subsequently largely discredited on the basis of faulty design that failed to control for difference in socioeconomic status between the monolingual and bilingual groups. Later studies have reversed the relationship, finding that if subjects were "balanced bilinguals" they generally demonstrated superiority on a number of types of tests over monolingual subjects matched on other variables except that of language (Peal and Lambert, 1962; Cummins and Gulutson, 1974; Iliams, 1976; Merino, 1975).

This study extends the findings of these other studies in that not only was the superiority of the bilingual group over the monolingual group established so far as "balanced bilinguals" were concerned, but even for children classified as "limited bilinguals." The study is also significant because the children represent a poverty-level group whereas most of the other research on this topic has involved subjects who came from the middle or upper class.

Findings Related to Whether Children Receive Bilingual Schooling in Communities that Encourage Language Shift (Washington State) or in Communities that Support Language Maintenance (Texas)

The greatest difference in test scores related to location was found for gains in English vocabulary. Children in the language shift location (Washington State) made much larger gains in English within the same period of attendance in the bilingual program than the children from the border town in Texas. The interaction between attendance and location was statistically significant at the 0.01 level.

Children in Washington State also made slightly higher scores in English reading than those in Texas, but the differences were not enough to be statistically significant.

There was relatively little difference in the pattern of gains or overall range of scores in Spanish vocabulary based on location (the sample was restricted to children whose primary language was Spanish), and what differences that existed were not statistically significant.

The language maintenance community, Texas, had children who scored significantly higher in math than the language shift communities in Washington State. The interaction between location and attendance was statistically significant at the 0.01 level for math scores.

In general, however, the bilingual program was found to mediate the effects of external factors that interact with an educational program. In Washington there is little community support for the maintenance of Spanish, but children in both Washington and Texas improved their Spanish over the baseline comparison group. In Texas there is relatively little incentive for learning English in a Texas border town in which nearly all communication is in Spanish, but children in both locations significantly improved their English, and the difference in performance between the locations became smaller for each older age group. Overall, the findings reported indicate that the scores of children in the two locations were more alike than they were different; the educational program itself appears to be primarily responsible for the gains children have made, and the program is capable of producing similar results even when there are great differences in the status of the minority language in given communities.

REFERENCES

Barlow, P. *Alice Independent School District Bilingual Education Project, 1975-76, Final Evaluation Report.* Duplicated. Alice, Tex., 1977.

Cohen, A.D. *A Sociolinguistic Approach to Bilingual Education.* Rowley, Mass.: Newbury House, 1975.

Collison, G.O. "Concept Formation in a Second Language: A Study of Ghanian School Children." *Harvard Educational Review* 44 (1974): 441-51.

Cummins, J. *The Influence of Bilingualism on Cognitive Growth: A Synthesis of Research Findings and Explanatory Hypotheses.* Working Papers on Bilingualism, no. 9. Toronto: Ontario Institute for Studies in Education, 1976. (ERIC ED 125 311).

_____ . *Linguistic Interdependence and the Educational Development of Bilingual Children.* Bilingual Education Paper Series, vol. 3, no. 2. Los Angeles: National Dissemination and Assessment Center, September 1979.

_____ , and Gulutson, M. "Some Effects of Bilingualism on Cognitive Functioning." In *Bilingualism, Biculturalism and Education,* edited by S. Carey. Edmonton: University of Alberta Press, 1974.

Darcy, N.T. "A Review of the Literature on the Effects of Bilingualism upon the Measure of Intelligence." *Journal of Genetic Psychology* 82 (1953): 21-57.

_____ . "Bilingualism and Intelligence: Review of a Decade of Research." *Journal of Genetic Psychology* 103 (1963): 259-82.

Engle, P.L. *The Use of Vernacular Languages in Education: Language Medium in Early School Years for Minority Language Groups.* Bilingual Education Series, no. 3. Arlington, Va.: Center for Applied Linguistics, 1975.

Gudschinsky, S. "Literacy in the Mother Tongue and Second Language Learning." Paper presented at the Conference on Child Language, 1971, Chicago.

Iliams, T.M. "Assessing the Scholastic Achievement and Cognitive Development of Bilingual and Monolingual Children." In *The Bilingual Child: Research and Analysis of Existing Educational Themes,* edited by A. Simões, Jr. New York: Academic Press, 1976.

Kyle, K. *Title VII Aprendemos en Dos Idiomas, Program Evaluation 1975-76, 861-HAS.* Duplicated. Corpus Christi, Tex., March 1976.

Lambert, W.E. "Culture and Language as Factors in Learning and Education." In *Education of Immigrant Students,* edited by A. Wolfgang. Toronto: Ontario Institute for Studies in Education, 1975.

_____ , and Tucker, G.R. *Bilingual Education of Children: The St. Lambert Experiment.* Rowley, Mass.: Newbury House, 1972.

Leyba, C.F. *Longitudinal Study, Title VII Bilingual Programs, Santa Fe Public Schools, Santa Fe, New Mexico.* Los Angeles: National Dissemination and Assessment Center, 1978.

Macnamara, J. *Bilingualism and Primary Education.* Edinburgh, Scotland: Edinburgh University Press, 1966.

Malherbe, E.G. *The Bilingual School: A Study of Bilingualism in South Africa.* London: Green, 1946.

Merino, B. "Early Bilingualism and Cognition: A Survey of the Literature." In *Perspectives on Chicano Education,* edited by T. Gonzales and S. Gonzales. Palo Alto, Calif.: Stanford University Press, 1975.

Modiano, N. *Indian Education in the Chiapas Highlands.* New York: Holt, Rinehart and Winston, 1973.

Nie, N.; Hull, C.H.; Jenkins, J.G.; Steingrenner, K.; and Bent, D.H. *Statistical Package for the Social Sciences.* 2d ed. New York: McGraw-Hill, 1970, 1975.

Paulston, C.B. *Ethnic Relations and Bilingual Education: Accounting for Contradictory Data.* Working Papers on Bilingualism, no. 6. Toronto: Ontario Institute for Studies in Education, 1975. (ERIC ED 125 253.)

Peal, E., and Lambert, W.E. "The Relation of Bilingualism to Intelligence." *Psychological Monographs* 76, no. 27 (1962).

Ramos, M.; Aguilar, J.; and Sibayan, B. *The Determination and Implementation of Language Policy.* Quezon City, Philippines: Oceana Publications, 1967.

Rosier, P., and Farella, M. "Bilingual Education at Rock Point—Some Early Results." *TESOL Quarterly* 10 (1976): 379-88.

Skutnabb-Kangas, T. *Language in the Process of Cultural Assimilation and Structural Incorporation of Linguistic Minorities.* Rosslyn, Va.: National Clearinghouse for Bilingual Education, 1979.

Troike, R.C. *Research Evidence for the Effectiveness of Bilingual Education.* Rosslyn, Va.: National Clearinghouse for Bilingual Education, 1978.

U.S., Commission on Civil Rights. *Mexican American Educational Series, Report II: The Unfinished Education.* Washington, D.C.: U.S. Government Printing Office, 1971.

Zappert, L.T., and Cruz, B.R. *Bilingual Education: An Appraisal of Empirical Research.* Berkeley, Calif.: Bay Area Bilingual Education League/Lau Center, 1977. (ERIC ED 153 758)

The Effect of the Language of Instruction on the Reading Achievement of Limited English Speakers in Secondary Schools

William A. Meléndez

Semifinalist, Outstanding Dissertations
National Advisory Council on Bilingual Education

Degree conferred May 1980
University of the Pacific
Stockton, California

Dissertation Committee:
Roger Reimer, *Chair*
Augustine García
Halvor Hansen
Fred Muskal
Randall Rockey

About the Author

Dr. William A. Meléndez is the Coordinator of the Migrant Education Program in Monterey County, California. He has been a teacher, a counselor, a site administrator, and a coordinator of ESEA Title VII Project Saber, a secondary bilingual-bicultural education program.

SUMMARY

The purpose of this study was to determine the effect that the language of instruction had on the English reading achievement of limited-English, dominant-Spanish-speaking students at secondary schools in five selected school districts in California.

Three pedagogical approaches in reading instruction for secondary-school-aged students were studied, namely, English language instruction, bilingual instruction, and Spanish language instruction. Pupils who received reading instruction in English learned reading skills and English, a compound task. Students taught bilingually learned reading skills in two languages, a compound task. Pupils taught in Spanish learned reading skills in a language already understood by them, focusing primarily on reading instruction, a single task.

The major finding of this study suggested that the linguistically distinct students' mother tongue, when used as an instructional vehicle in reading instruction, produced statistically significant English reading test score data. Students taught in Spanish did better in English reading than those students taught in English or in a bilingual mode.

A conclusion of this study identified the weakness of an educational system that denigrates the mother tongue of the linguistically distinct students in their education. This implication is especially important to those pedagogical practices currently used in the secondary schools in the United States.

INTRODUCTION

Limited- and non-English-speaking students have been "de-educated" of their language and culture in order to make them acceptable to the educational system in the United States. Although the Spanish language has been used in this country for centuries, each new Spanish-speaking generation must be "de-educated" of its mother tongue before formal education is generally allowed to begin. A conflict of cultures in the schools of the Southwest has taken place, where the teacher is the conqueror and the linguistically distinct student is the conquered (Steiner, 1969). Through this forced acculturation process, Spanish-speaking students have systematically rejected their families and themselves. With the eradication of the Spanish language and culture, students are prepared to become part of the dominant society.

Failure is a common bond that cements most of the culturally distinct minorities in the United States (Cordasco, 1968). A decade ago the Mexican American student in the Southwest was a negative statistic in the sense that nearly one million Spanish-speaking students did not complete the eighth grade (NEA, 1966). Ninety percent failed to graduate from high school (Chilcott, 1968). The first nationwide effort to trace educational achievement of the Hispanic population indicates that they are consistently below their contemporaries in the rest of the nation in reading, science, mathematics, social studies, and career education ("Hispanic Youth. . .," 1977).

The founders of the United States believed that the strength of the Republic rested upon a citizenry that was well educated. Their revolution was to predicate a country on the ideals of freedom, equality, and justice. Today, U.S. education is being called upon to aid the people in a renewed search for these ideals. Although education was to stress *Unum*, it has begun to give way to the forces of *Pluribus*, a political concept intended to further strengthen the Republic (Butts, 1976).

The goals of education have not changed drastically in the past sixty years. According to a recent report from the National Education Association, the "Seven Cardinal Principles" enumerated at the turn of the century by the Commission on the Reorganization of Secondary Education are valid today (Shane, 1976). In addition, there is a growing awareness that the student's mother tongue is the key to literacy (UNESCO, 1953).

LINGUISTICALLY DISTINCT STUDENTS

Teaching linguistically distinct students in a language that they do not understand traumatizes, demoralizes, and degrades them during the learning experience. Not only is the vehicle of instruction incomprehensible, but an additional burden is placed on the students when they must repudiate their cultural identity when "English only" rules are imposed. This pervasive condition places the students in a disadvantaged position which becomes increasingly pronounced during the educational years. Factors such as these reinforce the failure syndrome and many students leave school at an early age. The dropouts then become statistical references who had been underachievers, low performers, and poor readers (Ortega, 1976).

Thonis (1976), however, sees Spanish speakers as possessing strengths that benefit instruction. She suggests that these ethnically distinct children are generally cooperative, considerate, and capable, with an interest in helping others. These students enjoy classroom activities that promote success, and are able to set aside personal need in deference to the needs of others. Thonis also implies that ethnically distinct students respond to attention and affection, and that their reserved nature is often miscalculated by the uninitiated teacher.

Thonis also suggests that reading programs that were designed for native English speakers are totally unsuited to the reading needs of native speakers of Spanish, who have a different sound and symbol system which interferes with a second language. The grinding, corrosive effect of repeated failure and frustration has made reading an unsatisfactory experience for students whose literacy needs can best be met by instruction in their dominant language. The period of infancy, with thousands of hours of sound saturation, language models, and opportunities for imitation, provides the children with a linguistic system that has been internalized, and which should be used educationally. Like speakers of English, Spanish speakers have had to deal with oral language in the initial stages of development. During the educational progression the students require instruction in writing and reading skills.

Thonis (1976) suggests that for Spanish speakers the task of learning to read and write Spanish can be a most satisfying and productive endeavor, since the initial phase of communication skills, acquiring the oral language, has been thoroughly internalized. It is now a matter of adding a new dimension, the written representation of the spoken language. Instead of having to deal simultaneously with two or three unknowns, i.e., English speech, print, and attendant referents, students have only to memorize the visual symbols of the Spanish writing system and associate them with the auditory symbols of oral Spanish. An added advantage to Spanish speakers that is not available to speakers of English is that there is a regular and consistent relationship between written and spoken Spanish. The speech-print correlation, though not perfect, is dependable enough to create a sense of self-confidence in the students and belief in their own feelings of competence as readers.

Despite the conflicting data that exist on the optimum age for second language learning, there is reason to believe that students experience more interference between language systems if the second language is added before the first is completely developed (Saville-Troike, 1976). The role of the first language or mother tongue, sometimes referred to as the vernacular, is considered to be the irreplaceable instrument of education. Rodríguez Morales (1970) cites a number of authors on this issue: Dr. Frank L. Stoval points out that teaching in a language that is not the mother tongue produces confusion in the development of concepts, retards learning, and can be the cause of difficulty in expressing oneself for the rest of one's life. Dr. Michael West contends that the non-use of the vernacular brings about emotional instability, excessive negative behavior, artistic sterility, and a diminution of the creative power. Sir Henry Newbolt suggests that until the student has acquired a certain command of the mother tongue, no other language development is even possible. The noted Puerto Rican writer, Don Miguel Meléndez Muñoz, equally concerned about education in the mother tongue, states that teaching should be transmitted in the mother tongue and the study in the second language introduced only after the student has acquired a fundamental awareness of the mother tongue (Rodríguez Morales, 1970).

The findings of a study conducted in the highlands of Chiapas, Mexico, indicate that students who first learned to read in their mother tongue, before receiving instruction in a second language, read with greater comprehension in the second language than those who received all reading instruction in the second language (Modiano, 1968).

Other educators promote the use of the mother tongue because, beyond lessening scholastic retardation, it strengthens the bond between the home and the school. This minimizes the alienation of the family and linguistic community from the school community, which is the usual price for rejecting the mother tongue and subsequent assimilation into the dominant linguistic group. Developing strong literacy in the students' first language becomes a strong asset for them in adult life (Gaarder, 1975).

Bilingual education programs provide academic instruction in the mother tongue while they foster language development in the second language. These programs not only provide subject matter and concepts in the mother tongue and second language, but they also develop student confidence, self-assurance, and a positive identity with cultural heritage (Harvey, 1976).

Although the literature suggests that the mother tongue is essential to the educational and emotional development of limited-English-speaking students, the reality of a U.S. secondary education is that students must also have a strong command of English if the curriculum is to be open to them. Out of 200,832 teachers in California (Grant and Lind, 1977), there are approximately 2,500 certified bilingual teachers (Gettner, 1978), or 1.25 percent of the total teacher population. Given this information, it seems reasonable to consider the notion that students taught in the mother tongue will improve their chances in a comprehensive high school. Finally, research also indicates that there is a positive transfer of basic skills that are developed in the mother tongue to the language of the majority culture (Cziko, 1976).

STATEMENT OF THE PROBLEM

There continues to be a disproportionate number of limited-English-speaking students whose reading achievement scores are below the second quartile when measured by standardized, norm-referenced tests. In spite of current literature that suggests bilingual approaches to instruction are more effective, limited-English-speaking students are generally taught in English without the support and reinforcement of their mother tongue. It seems clear that research specific to the needs of limited-English-speaking students in the area of reading is important if an impact is to be made on the achievement levels of these students.

PURPOSE OF THE STUDY

The purpose of this study is to ascertain whether the use of the mother tongue as a vehicle of instruction is a more effective technique to teach reading to limited-English-speaking students at the secondary level than instruction in the language of the host culture.

PROCEDURES

The students included in this study were classified by school personnel as limited-English speakers if they met one of the following criteria. First, the students were classified as limited or non-English speakers during the October 1977 census in which the San Diego Observation Assessment Instrument, or any other instrument sanctioned by the California Department of Education, was employed. Second, the students had a home language other than English and had obtained grade equivalents in norm-referenced tests that placed them two or more years behind the norming population in reading or language tests. Third, the students were classified as limited or non-English speakers by other tests such as Basic Oral Language Test (BOLT), the Language Assessment Scales (LAS), the Basic Inventory of Natural Language (BINL), the Language Assessment Battery (LAB), or the InterAmerican Series of the Guidance Testing Associates.

Districts were selected from a list of secondary schools that offered bilingual instruction and who indicated a willingness to participate in the study. Reading, literacy classes, or content area reading classes taught in English, Spanish, or bilingually in Grades 7 through 10 were included in this study.

DEFINITIONS

- **Bilingual Education:** The use of two languages as a vehicle of instruction.

- **Language of the Host Culture:** The predominant language of a country whose language and/or culture differs from that of the immigrant, migrant, non- or limited-speaker.

- **Linguistically Distinct Student:** A non-pejorative phrase to identify a student who speaks a language other than English that is used to categorize the LES/NES student.

- **Limited English Speaker (LES):** A student whose mother tongue is other than English and who is demonstrably behind English-speaking peers in English language skills. (An inclusive phrase for the non-English speaker.)

- **Mother Tongue:** The student's first language, the dominant language, the language of the home, the vernacular, the native language.

RESEARCH DESIGN

In order to examine the effect that the language of instruction had on the English reading achievement of limited-English-speaking secondary students, a research design was developed that consisted of one independent variable and two dependent variables. The independent variable, instructional treatment, consisted of Treatment 1, English instruction; Treatment 2, bilingual instruction; and Treatment 3, Spanish instruction. The instructional treatment data were gathered from a classroom-level questionnaire as reported by teachers. (See the Appendix.) The dependent variables were English and Spanish reading achievement pretest and posttest scores which were used to assess reading ability in the English language and the Spanish language. In Figure 1, a graphic illustration of the research design is provided.

English/Spanish Reading Ability of LES/NES	Instructional Treatment		
	Treatment 1 English	Treatment 2 Bilingual	Treatment 3 Spanish
7-8 Grade	71	30	81
9-10 Grade	23	21	14

Figure 1
The Research Design

A general hypothesis of this study was that the English reading achievement of limited-English-speaking students would be improved significantly when they received instruction in Spanish as reading skills were being taught and learned. Specifically, the null hypotheses were:

Hypothesis 1. There are no significant differences in English reading achievement among limited-English-speaking students taught reading in English, bilingually, or in Spanish.

Hypothesis 2. There are no significant differences in Spanish reading achievement among limited-English-speaking students taught reading in English, bilingually, or in Spanish.

Hypothesis 3. There are no significant differences in English reading achievements between male and female students taught reading in the three treatment groups.

Hypothesis 4. There are no significant differences in Spanish reading achievement between male and female students taught reading in the three treatment groups.

The analysis of covariance (ANCOVA) and the post-hoc multiple comparison test, Scheffé, were used in the statistical treatment. The ANCOVA was used to test the null hypotheses. The Scheffé was used to determine which of the treatment groups differed significantly from the other groups. Tables were provided to indicate under what conditions English or Spanish reading achievement was affected by the instructional treatment. The ANCOVA was tested at the 0.10 level of significance. The Scheffé was tested at the 0.05 level of significance.

STATISTICAL ANALYSES

English and Spanish reading posttest means were analyzed to determine the effect of language on reading ability in the three instructional modes being studied.

Four hypotheses were tested by ANCOVA. The Scheffé procedure was used to compare the posttest means of the three treatment groups to ascertain which group produced significantly different reading achievement test-score means in English and in Spanish among limited-English-speaking secondary students.

In an analysis of the data with ANCOVA, as it pertained to the first and second hypotheses, the computations suggested that there were significantly different reading achievement posttest means in both English reading and Spanish reading. A rejection of Hypotheses 1 and 2 was based upon the data produced by the analysis of covariance. The treatment groups' posttest scores were also subjected to the Scheffé test. Students who received reading instruction in Spanish (Treatment 3), acquired significantly different test score means in English and Spanish reading achievement than those students in the other two treatment groups, namely English or bilingual instruction treatment groups. The Scheffé procedure identified the Spanish treatment group's Spanish and English reading test scores as significantly different from the other treatment groups.

When sex was considered, the English posttest means suggested that female subjects received significantly higher test-score means than male subjects. These data suggested that Hypothesis 3 should be rejected. Additionally, the Spanish posttest means suggested that female subjects had acquired significantly higher test-score means than male subjects, thus rejecting Hypothesis 4.

FINDINGS, CONCLUSIONS, AND IMPLICATIONS

A large percentage of the linguistically distinct student population have failed in the all-English curriculum of the comprehensive secondary school. These students entered the schools with skills that were cast aside for a preferred language. Their failure might be due in part to the fact that the attributes of the mother tongue were not fostered nor enhanced in the learning process. Linguistic chauvinism of this type has had a deleterious effect on the education of minority language pupils in the United States.

The linguistically distinct pupils' language is an important factor in their education. Use of the mother tongue to teach reading would promote reading readiness, an important preparation for the reading experience at any grade level. The mother tongues' use in early reading experiences allows for decoding of the printed word that closely resembles the spoken or heard word. This allows the students to learn reading without compounding the task with learning a second language. Additionally, because the grammatical rules governing the use of the language have already been internalized before the reading task is begun, the decoding of words, as well as determining the meaning of words would be promoted.

This study suggested that linguistically distinct students who were taught reading in their mother tongue did significantly better on the English reading achievement test than those students taught reading in English only or a bilingual mode. Submerging these students in the language of the host culture did not seem to improve their English reading achievement at the secondary level. The salient point of this research is that instruction in the mother tongue of the linguistically distinct students at the secondary level is essential for their continued progress in the total spectrum of the secondary-school curriculum. The effective acquisition of English reading skills, a basic goal of bilingual bicultural education is readily accomplished when a strong foundation in the mother tongue has been laid.

The inability or unwillingness of secondary-school districts to provide instruction in the mother tongue totally disregards the right to an equal educational opportunity. Ethnocentrism and language chauvinism do not allow for a rational educational approach. The lack of direction from boards of education or the lack of knowledge about educational research surrounding advances in bilingual bicultural education among teachers, administrators, or counselors are not valid excuses for preventing students from learning.

This study identified the weakness of an educational system that denigrates the mother tongue of its linguistically distinct pupils. The mother tongue is a primary source of strength that these pupils bring to the learning process. A potential effect of the neglect of the mother tongue is illiteracy or semilingualism, something that any society can ill afford.

APPENDIX
Secondary School Classroom Level Questionnaire in
Bilingual Education for Reading or Language Arts

Directions: Complete this questionnaire ONLY if you have normative test data, e.g., CTBS—English Reading or Language scores for your class.

Place a check (√) in the appropriate space for those statements that are TRUE and applicable to your class.

Fill out one questionnaire and test score sheet for each class.

The students are taught language arts or reading or
content area reading in a language other than English . . . .   1 ( )

The language other than English used is . . . . Spanish   2 ( )

                      Filipino   3 ( )

                      Chinese   4 ( )

          Other _____   5 ( )

My students have been classified as . . . limited English speakers   6 ( )

              fluent English speakers   7 ( )

          non-English speakers   8 ( )

The subject area that I teach, in the
language other than English, is . . . . Content Area Reading   9 ( )

                 Language Arts   10 ( )

                    Reading   11 ( )

The grade level for this class is. . . . . non-graded junior high   12 ( )

              non-graded senior high   13 ( )

                   seventh   14 ( )

                    eighth   15 ( )

                    ninth   16 ( )

                     tenth   17 ( )

                  eleventh   18 ( )

                  twelfth   19 ( )

The class period(s) spent in the
subject area is (are) . . . . one period   20 ( )

                  two periods   21 ( )

           three periods   22 ( )

         more than three   23 ( )

I spend the following percentage of time, in
the language other than English, when I teach . . . . 0%   24 ( )

          25% - 50%   25 ( )

        75% - 100%   26 ( )

I am interested in the results of this research
Please send me a summary of the finished study . . . .   27 ( )

REFERENCES

Butts, R. Freeman. "The Search for Purpose in American Education." *Today's Education* 65 (March-April 1976): 77.

Chilcott, John H. *Readings in Socio-Cultural Foundations of Education.* Belmont, Calif.: Wadsworth, 1968.

Cordasco, Francesco. "The Challenge of Non-English Speaking Children in American Schools." *Schools and Society* 96 (March 1968): 200.

Cziko, Gary A. "The Effects of Language Sequencing on the Development of Bilingual Reading Skills." *Canadian Modern Review* 32 (May 1976): 534-39.

Gaarder, A. Bruce. "Organization of the Bilingual School." In *A Mosaic of Readings in Bilingual Education, English-Spanish,* edited by William A. Manning. San Jose, Calif.: Spartan Bookstore, 1975.

Gettner, Gustavo. Director, Bilingual Section of the California Commission of Teacher Preparation and Licensing. Letter, 21 June 1978.

Grant, W. Vance, and Lind, C. George. *Digest of Education Statistics.* Washington, D.C.: U.S. Government Printing Office, 1977.

Harvey, Curtis. "General Descriptions of Bilingual Programs That Meet Students' Needs." In *Bilingual Schooling in the United States,* edited by Francesco Cordasco. New York: Webster Division, McGraw-Hill, 1976.

"Hispanic Youth Consistently below Contemporaries in Education Achievement." *NAEP Newsletter* (June 1977).

Modiano, Nancy. "National or Mother Language in Beginning Reading: A Comparative Study." *Research in the Teaching of English* 2 (April 1968): 32-43.

National Education Association (NEA), Department of Rural Education. "The Invisible Minority: Report of the NEA-Tucson Survey on the Teaching of Spanish to the Spanish Speaking." Washington, D.C.: National Education Association, 1966.

Ortega, Phillip D. "The Education of Mexican Americans." In *The Chicanos: Mexican American Voices,* edited by Ed Ludwig and Mames Santibanez. Baltimore: Penguin Books, 1971.

Rodríguez Morales, Luis M. "The Vernacular in Teaching." In *Politics and Education in Puerto Rico,* edited by Erwin H. Epstein. Metuchen, N.J.: Scarecrow Press, 1970.

Saville-Troike, Muriel. "Bilingual Children: A Resource Document." In *Bilingual Schooling in the United States,* edited by Francesco Cordasco. New York: Webster Division, McGraw-Hill, 1976.

Shane, Harold G. "The Seven Cardinal Principles Revisited." *Today's Education* 65 (September-October 1976): 59.

Steiner, Stan. *La Raza: The Mexican Americans.* New York: Harper and Row, 1969.

Thonis, Eleanor W. *Literacy for America's Spanish Speaking Children.* Reading Aids Series. Newark, Del.: International Reading Association, 1976.

United Nations Educational, Scientific, and Cultural Organization. *The Use of Vernacular Languages in Education.* Paris: UNESCO, 1953.

Variation in Language Use Patterns Across Different Group Settings in Two Bilingual Second Grade Classrooms

Robert D. Milk

Semifinalist, Outstanding Dissertations
National Advisory Council on Bilingual Education

Degree conferred October 1980
Stanford University School of Education
Stanford, California

Dissertation Committee:
Robert Politzer, *Chair*
Arnulfo Ramírez
Lyn Corno

About the Author

Dr. Robert D. Milk is Assistant Professor in the Division of Bicultural-Bilingual Studies at the University of Texas at San Antonio. He was previously coordinator of the Special Language Program and instructor in the Linguistics Department at Stanford University. He has published several articles on bilingual education and language acquisition.

SUMMARY

The primary purpose of this study was to obtain natural, descriptive information on language use patterns in bilingual classrooms, and to analyze this information in relation to the types of grouping decisions that are commonly made by teachers.

Students from two bilingual second-grade classrooms were tape-recorded for one full day. The students' speech was then analyzed with respect to three descriptors of language use: (1) how much they used English and Spanish, (2) the complexity of their speech, and (3) for what purposes they used the two languages of the classroom.

The most striking finding of this study was that students rarely used their weaker language, except during formal second language instruction. A second finding was that the group setting in which student interactions took place had a direct effect on language use patterns. Two important conclusions can be drawn from these findings: first, that decisions made by teachers with regard to grouping strategies *can* have a direct effect on student language use; and second, that teachers need to develop grouping strategies that will more effectively encourage interaction among students from different language dominance backgrounds.

STATEMENT OF THE PROBLEM

Since the enactment in 1968 of Title VII of the Elementary and Secondary Education Act (ESEA), bilingual education has experienced steady growth, in terms of both finding support at the federal level and the total number of programs initiated in communities across the nation. Like most educational innovations that are initiated without a solid research base to guide implementation, bilingual bicultural education (BBE) has often been forced to adopt a trial-and-error approach, resulting in highly uneven results across different settings.

The feeling is widespread among BBE practitioners that the lack of a strong research tradition is the single greatest obstacle to improvement of program quality. In the words of one California advocate (Cervantes, 1977, p. 8), research is the "Achilles' heel" of BBE, and "it is doubtful that significant progress can be made unless more serious substantive research is undertaken."

The bulk of research that has been carried out in this area is outcome oriented. In a recent review of social science research on BBE, Fishman (1977) mentions only one study that contained data on classroom processes—the 1975 U.S. Commission on Civil Rights (USCCR) classroom interaction study—and this study was not conducted in bilingual classrooms, but, rather, in single-medium classrooms. In the same volume, Mehan (1977) decries the absence of process-oriented studies in bilingual education. Those few studies that *have* examined classroom processes have tended to use quantitative observation approaches, such as the Flanders-type interaction analysis used in the USCCR study. This type of approach, while valuable in identifying potential problem areas, provides little qualitative, descriptive information of the kind needed to address the question of improving classroom instruction. Mehan advocates a more ethnographic approach based on intensive classroom observation, and suggests that this approach be used to "compare the language that students use in various classroom situations. These comparisons would show the situations in which students use their first and second language, with what degree of skill, and when they switch between languages" (p. 87).

In the context of BBE, one area of research that needs to be explored is that of classroom language. Given that the most salient distinguishing characteristic of bilingual education is its use of two languages for instruction, the relative lack of descriptive information about how children use language in bilingual classrooms represents a serious void. Although the language use of children in classrooms has received a fair amount of attention over the past decade (Bellack, et al., 1966; Barnes and Rosen, 1971; Rosen and Rosen, 1973; Sinclair and Coulthard, 1975; Barnes and Todd, 1977), no in-depth descriptive studies aimed at examining the use of two languages by children in bilingual classrooms have been performed to date.

PURPOSE OF THE STUDY

Even a brief survey of the literature on bilingual bicultural education quickly reveals the extent to which BBE has different meanings for different people. To many, it means simply any educational program designed for children who are "bilingual." To others, it means a temporary program that provides an effective and painless bridge to English instruction. For the majority of BBE advocates, however, bilingual education implies both a strong commitment to the children's home cultures, as well as the development and maintenance of two languages. For many parents who have supported bilingual programs, it is this goal of dual language development that has led them to select bilingual education as an educational alternative for their children.

In implementing bilingual programs for which dual language development is a primary goal, certain central questions emerge: How can the bilingual classroom be structured in a way that will maximize the dual language development of all students, regardless of language background? To what extent can routine classroom activity be conceptualized within a framework that encourages students to interact in their weaker language? Does this, in fact, occur naturally in the classroom, or must the teacher take specific steps to encourage students to engage in this type of interaction? Are bilingual classrooms providing the necessary conditions for second language acquisition to take place?

These questions are becoming increasingly relevant, in light of accumulating evidence regarding the extremely limited results that can be obtained in the lower elementary grades from fifteen to twenty minutes of daily second language instruction. Moreover, based on the results of recent second language acquisition studies, it appears that children must receive a certain amount of input in the target language as a necessary (though not sufficient) condition for acquiring that language. Determining the degree to which such input may or may not be present in the classroom being studied is a major concern of this study.

In order to better address issues that are relevant to practitioners, the research questions in this study have been formulated within a framework that suggest alternative courses of action for practitioners—viz., the effect of teacher grouping strategies on student language use patterns. Decisions regarding optimal grouping arrangements are among the most fundamental that teachers must make on a continuous basis. These decisions take on even greater importance in bilingual classrooms, where teachers must deal with different groups based on language dominance criteria for reading, language arts, second language instruction, and subject area instruction. A common practice in bilingual classrooms is, for the sake of administrative efficiency (as well as student performance, in many cases), to seat children for the full day according to language dominance. Although this greatly facilitates teacher management tasks, particularly in assuring a smooth transition from one activity to another, the consequences for second language development may be quite significant. In the absence of natural input based on real communication encounters in the second language, the primary vehicle for learning the second language becomes, by default, formal second language instruction. From all available evidence, this vehicle may not, in and of itself, be sufficient to promote significant development in the second language of a child.

Ultimately, of course, the extent to which children develop in their second language is likely to depend more on factors that exist outside the classroom than on what happens within—the language use patterns within the children's homes and the community at large will probably have a significant impact on the children's ultimate language development (Rubin, 1977). Though teachers have no control over these larger societal forces, they can and do control grouping strategies in classrooms. The focus of this study, consequently, is restricted to language use issues at a microsociolinguistic level, not because patterns of language use at a more macro level are deemed unimportant to bilingual education practitioners, but, rather, because the immediate concern here is with variables that can be manipulated directly by the classroom teacher.

In very broad terms, the primary purpose of this study was *to obtain natural, descriptive information on language use patterns in bilingual classrooms, and to analyze this information in relation to the types of grouping decisions that are commonly made by teachers.* At a global level, the kinds of questions being explored in this study included:

1. Do the language use patterns of students in bilingual classrooms vary depending on the group settings in which the interaction takes place? If differences are evident, what implications do these differences have for language development in each of the two languages of the classroom?

2. Is there an interaction between student language characteristics (i.e., "language dominance") and group setting?

SAMPLING

Selection of Classes/Schools

The investigation was carried out in a large, rapidly growing city in northern California. Within the city as a whole, over 35 percent of the students are of Hispanic descent. The schools are highly segregated, and in the city's largest school district, sixteen of the fifty-one elementary schools have student populations of over 60 percent minority origin.

Within this city, bilingual education programs are found primarily in schools that have a substantial minority population. As a rule, they tend to appear in schools that serve predominantly low socioeconomic status communities, and the vast majority of students enrolled in Spanish-English bilingual programs in this area are of Mexican ancestry.

Based on these factors (ethnic background of students and socioeconomic status of the surrounding community) a "typical" elementary school district containing bilingual education programs was identified. (For the purpose of this study, *bilingual education program* was defined as a program of instruction that uses two languages, one of which is English, as media of instruction for all or part of the curriculum.) The two sample classrooms were selected systematically from among the bilingual classrooms in this district.

Selection of the two second-grade classrooms for participation in the study was based on two criteria: (1) that they be located in a school that contained a fully functioning bilingual program for at least Grades K-4, and (2) that the participating teachers be experienced bilingual teachers, judged as "highly effective" by both their principals and by the district's bilingual resource teachers. Based on these criteria, two second-grade classrooms were selected.

Selection of Students

Twelve students were randomly selected from each of the two classrooms for participation in the study, with four students per class (two male and two female) representing each of the three language dominance groups (Spanish dominant, balanced bilingual, English dominant).

The whole issue of language dominance is a problematic one in BBE. There is some question as to whether the concept of dominance is either valid or useful in describing the relative language proficiency of bilingual children (Duncan and DeAvila, 1979). Nevertheless, because this study was conceived as a natural study that would attempt to describe classrooms as they functioned in the "real world," and because "language dominance" was the most common means of classifying students at the time of the study, the trimodal classification used by the target school district was incorporated into the design. According to this system, children were classified as belonging to one of three language dominance groups:

Spanish dominant: The child can function effectively in the classroom in Spanish, but not in English.

English dominant: The child can function effectively in the classroom in English, but not in Spanish.

Balanced bilingual: The child can function effectively in the classroom in both Spanish and English.

The basis for classifying students was the Language Assessment Battery (LAB), which was administered to the students in English and Spanish in September. The cutoff point for establishing ability to "function effectively" was the twentieth percentile rank. (The LAB is normed on monolingual populations.) It should be noted that, given this exceedingly low cutoff point, "balanced bilinguals" did not, in fact, need to be "balanced" in order to be so classified. As it turned out, in this study all of the "balanced bilinguals" had clearly identifiable "stronger" and "weaker" languages.

Each of the participating students was recorded during one full day of class.

PROCEDURES

The design of the study required an extensive period of observation; consequently, arrangements were made for the investigator to be present in the classroom as a nonparticipant observer between late September and early December. The basic procedure included two basic stages:

Stage One: An intensive observational stage to determine in what types of group settings discourse took place, as well as to gain total familiarity with classroom procedures and participants prior to actual recording.

Stage Two: Based on the information obtained in Stage One, and taking into account those factors related to group composition that would most affect language use, representative interaction settings for obtaining recorded samples were identified. Natural audio recordings were then obtained of students as they carried out their normal class routine.

The prevalent group interaction settings that were identified during Stage One were: (1) large group, (2) small group, (3) teacher-directed, and (4) individual work.

In order to minimize the obtrusiveness of the recording procedure, two or three children were asked to wear a vest each day. One of the vests contained an inner pocket within which a small wireless microphone was placed. The recording equipment was set up in a corner of the classroom. The investigator was present during all recording in order to take down extensive notes regarding the context of each utterance by the target children. The children were aware of the fact that they were being recorded, and were allowed to play with the equipment. The novelty of the procedure wore off after a couple of weeks (prior to the collection of the language samples), and the influence of the recording procedure on the children's language behavior was estimated as being minimal.

The audio tapes obtained over a two-month period from procedures described above served as the primary data base. In addition, the observation notes were used wherever appropriate to assist in the interpretation of the data.

CRITERION VARIABLES

Three criterion variables were selected to measure language use. The first involved amount of talk in the two languages of the classroom, and was obtained using stopwatches. The second variable was complexity of speech, and was determined by performing a T-unit analysis of student utterances. The third aspect of language use examined was language functions, focusing on the uses to which the two languages of the classroom were put. A speech act category system developed by Wood et al. (1977) was used to code student utterances as to their function.

RESEARCH DESIGN

For purposes of analysis, the original 3x2x9 quasi-experimental design (language dominance, sex, group setting) was modified to allow for two global group setting comparisons: group size (large group versus small group) and instructional mode (teacher directed versus individual work). The two 3x2x2 modified designs can be illustrated in Figure 1.

ANALYSIS OF DATA

For inferential statistics to be appropriately applied, the sample under study had to be representative of the population at large. Since random sampling was not possible, this was clearly not the case. Though students within classrooms were selected at random, neither the classroom/school combinations nor the district were randomly selected. Moreover, even if the children in these classrooms could have been considered in some way "typical" of second-grade children in bilingual classrooms, bilingual programs vary radically on such a multitude of factors that generalizability based on results found in only two classrooms becomes a very dubious proposition.

The data analysis approach used in this study involved imposing the two 3x2x2 post hoc designs on each criterion variable. Because of small sample size and the quasi-experimental nature of the designs, group means were compared to overall standard deviations to determine "effect size." Cohen (1969) describes what is meant by "effect size":

> Without intending any necessary implication of causality, it is convenient to use the phrase "effect size" to mean "the *degree* to which the phenomenon is present in the population," or "the degree to which the null hypothesis is false" .... When the null hypothesis is false, it is false to some specific degree, i.e., *the effect size (ES) is some specific nonzero value in the population.* The larger this value, the greater the *degree* to which the phenomenon under study is manifested. (Cohen, 1969, pp. 9-10, author's emphasis)

The formula for calculating effect size (d) is:

$$d = \frac{\text{mean}_1 - \text{mean}_2}{\text{standard deviation pooled}}$$

Cohen goes on to provide guidelines as to what might be considered "small" (d = 0.2), "medium" (d = 0.5), or "large" (d = 0.8) effect sizes. Although these guidelines are essentially arbitrary and will necessarily vary depending on the nature of the specific research problem, they appear to be meaningful for the type of data being dealt with in this study.

The strategy used in analyzing the data, consequently, was to identify effect sizes that were in the medium or high range (i.e., d = 0.50 or greater), in an effort to discover patterns that, when combined with the observational data collected over the course of the study, provided insights into student language use that seemed pedagogically significant.

MAIN FINDINGS

The data analysis revealed differences in student language use patterns both between classrooms and within classrooms. Significant differences were found between classes in amount of talk by students in their dominant language. In addition, the classroom that had the most student talk also had more complex student utterances, as well as a more balanced functional allocation of Spanish and English.

Within-class differences were found among the three language dominance groups. Balanced bilinguals used their "weaker" language more than

Group Size Comparison

	Language Dominance					
	Spanish dominant		Balanced bilingual		English dominant	
Group Setting	M	F	M	F	M	F
Large group						
Small group						

Instructional Mode Comparison

	Language Dominance					
	Spanish dominant		Balanced bilingual		English dominant	
Group Setting	M	F	M	F	M	F
Teacher directed						
Individual work						

M = male
F = female

Figure 1

the other students, although none of the students used their weaker language to as great an extent as expected. Other differences unique to each classroom were found.

Within-class differences were also found across group settings. In Class P, the highest proportion of academic talk occurred in small-group settings, whereas in Class Q it occurred in the teacher-directed setting. For the dominant language of students, there was more talk in the small groups than in the large groups.

CONCLUSIONS AND IMPLICATIONS

Perhaps the most striking finding of this study is that *the weaker language of all students, including balanced bilinguals, was infrequently used in the classroom for natural communication.* This finding is of considerable interest, given that the bilingual programs in these two schools placed an emphasis on bilingualism as a goal. There are two factors that seemed to mitigate against extensive use of the weaker language in these classrooms:

1. Grouping strategies used by the teachers mitigated against significant interaction across language dominance groups in these classrooms. Students were seated according to their reading group. These seating patterns, which effectively separated English-dominant and Spanish-dominant students, were maintained throughout most of the day.

2. There appeared to be an implicit assumption on the part of the teachers that second language acquisition takes place naturally in bilingual classrooms without any need for conscious planning. It is unlikely, however, that this acquisition can take place in any meaningful way in the absence of significant language input. As long as there is only minimal opportunity or need for children of contrasting language dominance backgrounds to interact in the classroom, it is not likely that much input in the weaker language will, in fact, be provided.

Major implications for educational practice can be drawn from the finding that the weaker language is infrequently used in those classrooms. To achieve more extensive use of the weaker language in bilingual classrooms, teachers can:

1. Develop grouping strategies that provide both the opportunity and the need for the weaker language of students to be used for social-interactive purposes.

2. Teachers must build second language development activities into their daily lesson plans, above and beyond what is done formally in the English as a second language/Spanish as a second language component of the program. There are several possibilities here, ranging from informal development of the weaker language during subject matter instruction, to problem-solving activities using small groups composed of students from different language dominance backgrounds.

A second conclusion that can be drawn from the study is that *group setting does, in fact, have an effect on language use.* Numerous differences were reported related to language use in contrasting group settings. The effect of group setting on language use seems to be mediated by teaching style. In Classroom P, where students were trained to work together in small groups, academic talk was most prevalent in small groups. In Classroom Q, where the teacher favored direct teaching as the primary means for transmitting knowledge, the highest proportion of academic talk occurred in the teacher-directed instructional mode. The effect of group setting on language use also seemed to be mediated by language dominance—what was true for the dominant language was often not true for the weaker language. For example, in Classroom P the dominant language was used with most frequency in the small-group setting, while the weaker language was used with most frequency in the large-group setting.

Despite these mediating factors, a consistent finding throughout was that *small-group settings seemed to provide a highly favorable context for language use.* In both classrooms, there was more talk in the small-group setting, as well as a higher frequency of speech acts. Another implication related to group setting is that excessive teacher control of student talk may have negative effects on oral language development. In Classroom Q, the range of speech acts was broader during individual work than during teacher-directed instruction.

A final implication is that *bilingual programs demonstrate a tremendous potential for effective second language development.* The basis for this judgment is the extent to which students in these classrooms used their weaker language for a variety of different functions. Despite the small quantity of talk in the weaker language, an examination of the range and content of that talk reveals that fully one-half (two-thirds in the case of Classroom Q) of talk in the weaker language involved the major communicative functions, whereas less than one-third was of the pseudocommunicative type (e.g., rehearsal speech) that typically predominates during formal second language instruction.

REFERENCES

Barnes, D.; Britton, J.; and Rosen, H. *Language, the Learner and the School.* Harmondsworth, England: Penguin, 1971.

Barnes, D., and Todd, F. *Communication and Learning in Small Groups.* London: Routledge and Kegan Paul, 1977.

Bellack, A.; Hyman, R.; Smith, F.; and Kliebard, H. *The Language of the Classroom.* New York: Teachers College Press, 1966.

Cervantes, R. *Research and Evaluation: The Achilles' Heel of Bilingual-Bicultural Education.* Sacramento, Calif.: State Department of Education, 1977.

Cohen, J. *Statistical Power Analysis for the Behavioral Sciences.* New York: Academic, 1969.

Duncan, S., and DeAvila, E. "Bilingualism and Cognition: Some Recent Findings." *NABE Journal* IV, no. 1 (Fall 1979): 15-50.

Fishman, J. "The Social Science Perspective." In *Bilingual Education: Current Perspectives,* vol. 1. Arlington, Va.: Center for Applied Linguistics, 1977.

Rosen, C., and Rosen, H. *The Language of Primary School Children.* Harmondsworth, England: Penguin, 1973.

Rubin, J. "Bilingual Education and Language Planning." In *Frontiers of Bilingual Education,* edited by B. Spolsky and R. Cooper. Rowley, Mass.: Newbury House, 1977.

Sinclair, J., and Coulthard, M. *Towards an Analysis of Discourse: The English Used by Teachers and Pupils.* London: Oxford University Press, 1975.

Wood, B., et al., eds. *Development of Functional Communication Competencies, Prekindergarten to Grade 6.* Urbana, Ill.: ERIC Clearinghouse on Reading and Communication Skills, 1977.

A Study of Standardized Language Dominance Tests and Their Correlation with Bilingual Judges' Opinions

Rosa Quezada

Semifinalist, Outstanding Dissertations
National Advisory Council on Bilingual Education

Degree conferred May 1980
University of Connecticut School of Education
Storrs, Connecticut

Dissertation Committee:
Mark R. Shibles, *Chair*
Gerald Rowe
Robert Gable

Copyright © 1981 by Rosa A. Quezada

About the Author

Dr. Rosa Quezada is assistant to the dean at the University of Connecticut's School of Education. She has also been a bilingual consultant with the Connecticut Staff Development Cooperative and a bilingual field agent with the New England Program in Teacher Education. Her publications include articles on testing and desegregation.

SUMMARY

This study determined to what extent and in what manner language dominance can be predicted by language dominance tests. Specifically, the relationship between the opinion of bilingual experts about language dominance and selected measures of language dominance were examined. A randomly selected sample of Spanish-surnamed children in Grades 1-3 were identified from three Connecticut communities. Their scores on group and individual tests of language dominance and a language survey were compared to bilingual expert opinion regarding each student's dominance. This study provides insight into the problem of identifying language dominance in bilingual students.

BACKGROUND

During the past twenty years much attention has focused on issues related to equal educational opportunity. One area that has received particular attention has been bilingual education. In the United States, bilingual bicultural education increasingly is used in teaching children whose dominant language is other than English. As we enter the 1980s, the numbers of such children (specifically Spanish surnamed) will continue to grow, possibly making this group the largest of minorities in the United States. It is becoming increasingly important, then, to determine the theoretical basis for bilingual bicultural programs. In addition, there is a major need to reach agreement on those approaches that meet the unique needs of this particular group of children.

Expanding resources have been allocated to bilingual programs by both federal and state government agencies. This has led in turn to expansion of legislated mandates regarding the processes used by local education agencies for selecting students who will participate in such programs. In both federal and state mandates reference is made to language dominance or language proficiency. These terms form the basis for judgments regarding eligibility of students to receive bilingual education. However, severe problems have emerged in developing definitions, methods, and instruments to measure a child's language dominance.

REVIEW OF THE LITERATURE

This study was undertaken to center on the specific problems in bilingual education to identify a reliable, as well as efficient means to determine which Spanish-surnamed children are Spanish- or English-dominant. Surname surveys, dominance rating scales, and teacher observations have been used frequently in language dominance assessment and subsequently have been found to be vague, indirect techniques which provide insufficient information regarding a child's actual communicative competence (Zirkel, 1976).

Counts of grammatical rules observed in transcribed speech (Genesee, 1975) as well as a combination of multiple measures to determine language dominance (Silverman and Russell, 1977) have been attempted. More effective procedures for defining a child's linguistic dominance include parallel testing (Zirkel, 1976), specially designed instruments whose components integrate interviews, story telling, and question-answer methods with language repetition and completion exercises (Silverman and Russell, 1976), and Hunt's Terminable-Unit (T-Unit) (Maurice and Roy, 1976).

However, other experts in the field have concluded that language tests based on the above linguistic criteria for predicting language dominance are inadequate (Bordie, 1976). Further, Spolsky (1972) and Mackey (1972) indicate that many scales which are employed for such purposes "presuppose standard units of measure which do not exist, and valid procedures for their delineation" (Mackey, 1972).

Finally, there are strong doubts that language dominance can realistically be measured. As one study claims: "The construct of language dominance is a legal and political rather than a linguistic, educational, or psychological construct" (Silverman and Russell, 1977).

The reviewed studies have points of agreement. First, in order to measure language dominance, social contexts must be taken into consideration. It is not enough to measure a child's linguistic competence in the domain of the educational setting (Zirkel, 1974). What happens in the home, in church, as well as on the playground must be investigated in order to obtain a clearer picture of what language the child functions best in (Dubois, 1974; Macnamara, 1967). Also, it appears that several of the studies agree that language dominance cannot be measured by just one instrument (Zirkel, 1974; Silverman and Russell, 1977).

The main point of disagreement in the above-mentioned studies is exactly how to determine language dominance. Some researchers focused on direct measures of testing language dominance such as word naming, word association (Cooper, 1969), syntax (Oller, 1966), vocabulary, sentence length (Politzer, 1974), and word counts (Cooper, 1969; Spilka, 1976). Others were more inclined to use direct measures such as questionnaires (Cohen, 1975), inventories (Melear, 1974), and teacher judgments.

The studies indicate that many areas of language dominance are yet to be explored. These include issues such as investigating the similarities and differences of first and second language acquisition (Paulston, 1974; Politzer, 1974). Another major issue seems to be that of how exactly one can measure language dominance (Bordie, 1976), and, finally, if language dominance is measurable (Silverman and Russell, 1977).

STATEMENT OF THE PROBLEM

The major problem of this study was to determine the extent and manner through which language dominance can be predicted by language dominance tests. Specifically, the relationship between bilingual judges' opinions about language dominance and selected measures of language dominance on the following tests was studied:

1. The Crane Oral Dominance Test (and its accompanying questionnaire)
2. Pupil Questionnaire for Language Dominance Survey (adaptation of Lau Survey)
3. Inter-American Test of General Abilities (oral vocabulary subtest).

Since it is neither realistic nor economical to assume that trained bilingual experts will be available or that school systems will be able to provide such services for the determination of language dominance, the use of a standardized test is an efficient, practical alternative. It was assumed that the test that established the highest correlation with the expert opinions could be utilized or compared with existing norms to make a placement procedure in bilingual programs more accurate.

The need to answer the following research questions was raised as a result of the problem statement:

1. What is the relationship between group-administered tests of language dominance and bilingual judges' opinion?
2. What is the relationship between individually administered tests of language dominance and bilingual judges' opinion?
3. What is the relationship between language surveys used to determine language dominance and bilingual judges' opinion?
4. What is the relative efficacy of group and individual language dominance tests and language dominance survey forms in predicting language dominance as classified by bilingual experts?

SAMPLING

Three school systems in Connecticut with high percentages of Spanish-surnamed students participated in this investigation. Participating school districts identified their Spanish-surnamed children in Grades 1-3. Fifty percent of the students identified as Spanish surnamed were then randomly selected for participation in this study in two of the three districts. This stratified random sampling was done to assure that students were selected who reflected variation in degrees of English and Spanish dominance. In the third district, all fourteen Hispanic students in that school district in Grades 1-3 were included in the study.

The sample was selected for several reasons. The Hispanic students selected are representative of the Hispanic student population that actually exists throughout Connecticut. The parallels between socioeconomic levels, grade levels, and ethnic backgrounds of the sample and the population assure the external validity of the study. The majority of these students statewide are concentrated at the elementary level. The selection of two urban centers and one rural center assured that communities where most Hispanic students in Connecticut are located would be represented in the sample. The final sample included 123 students in three communities. These students were in fourteen different schools within the school districts studied.

DESIGN

In this research nonparametric statistics were selected for analysis. Since no real way to measure language dominance has been identified, the three instruments used in this study could not be subjected to parametric procedures. While each of the instruments placed students into categories of English dominant, Spanish dominant, or bilingual, no interval scale composed of equal units existed for the instruments used in this study. While degrees of dominance within each of the three identified language dominance ratings can be placed on an ordinal scale, the original categories, in effect, can only be considered on a nominal scale. The categories are based upon certain qualitative differences. However, these differences cannot be ranked in any type of order. Popham and Sirotnik (1973) suggest that "unless data have been measured on a scale of at least interval strength, parametric techniques. . . should not be used."

The basic assumption underlying the use of nonparametric statistics in this research is that these statistics are appropriate for use with data that have been measured on nominal, or classificatory scales. Popham and Sirotnik (1973) suggest that this type of data "cannot on any logical basis, be ordered numerically, hence there is no possibility of using parametric statistical tests which require numerical data."

One of the oldest problems in descriptive statistics is that of indexing the strength of statistical association between qualitative attributes. Due to the nature of this study it was necessary to determine the strength of association between judges' opinions regarding students' language dominance and specific tests used to predict this dominance.

Although a number of simple and meaningful indices exist to describe association in a fourfold table, this problem grows more complex for larger tables. In this study the tables were, in fact, more complex. Three rows and three columns were needed due to the three language categories included in the assessment of language dominance. Downie and Heath (1974) suggest that one approach to the problem of describing association in complex tables rests with predictive association. Association between categorical attributes is indexed by the reduction in the probability of error in prediction afforded by knowing the status of the individual on one of the attributes.

Cramer's statistic was used in this research as a description of apparent strength of association in the sample. Cramer's statistic "must be between 0, reflecting complete independence, and 1, showing complete dependence of the attributes. The statistical significance of Cramer's statistic may be determined by testing the significance of the chi square statistic" (Downie and Heath, 1974, p. 203). In order to measure the predictive association for categorical data, Goodman and Kruskal developed an index of predictive association. This index is called Lambda (Downie and Heath, 1974, p. 248). In this study, research questions 1 through 4 were tested through the use of correlations Lambda and Cramer's V. In addition percentages of agreement were calculated in relation to each of the four research questions.

INSTRUMENTATION

Three categories of language dominance instruments were used in this study: (1) tests administered to subjects as a group, (2) tests administered to the subjects individually, and (3) sociolinguistic questionnaires. As an example of a group-administered test of language dominance, the vocabulary section of the Inter-American Test of General Abilities was administered to the subjects. This test consists of vocabulary words or expressions dictated by the test administrator; the child then marks the appropriate corresponding object in a row of pictures. The test was administered first in Spanish, then in English. Test questions were equivalent in level of difficulty in the two languages. This test measures the students' ability to comprehend a spoken word in either Spanish or English and then locate the corresponding picture on the test sheet.

The second test category attempts to classify students' language dominance through individual assessment in each of the languages to be tested. The Crane Test presents a series of words to the student that he or she must repeat. Auditory memory rather than actual oral language comprehension is the basis for making dominance decisions in this test.

The third type of assessment was made through the use of sociolinguistic questionnaires. In these instruments information gleaned from the students regarding language use outside the school is the basis for determining their language dominance. Both the Pupil Questionnaire for Language Dominance and the Optional Questionnaire section of the Crane Oral Dominance test were used as examples of sociolinguistic questionnaires.

PROCEDURES

To implement this research project tests of language dominance used in Connecticut were identified. This was verified by contacting directors of bilingual programs in communities offering programs of bilingual education as well as state Education Department consultants. The tests found to be used most widely and subsequently selected for inclusion in the study were the Crane Oral Dominance Test (with accompanying questionnaire), the InterAmerican Test of General Abilities (Oral Vocabulary section), and the Pupil Questionnaire for Language Dominance Survey.

School systems in Connecticut with high percentages of Spanish-surnamed students were then invited to participate in this investigation. Three districts were finally included in the research. Lists of all Spanish-surnamed students enrolled in each of the districts were forwarded to the researcher. Each student was assigned a number and through the use of a table of random numbers, the sample was selected.

Upon securing parental permission for inclusion in the study, each of the students included in the sample was interviewed. The purpose of this interview was to secure samples of students' language to be rated by the three bilingual judges. Students spent approximately ten minutes with the bilingual interviewer. Speech was elicited through the use of a free conversation approach. On occasion the interviewer prompted conversation by posing open-ended questions to the subject. For example, "What do you like to do after school? Do you help your mother at home? What do you like best about school? What is your favorite television show?" The first five minutes of the interview were conducted in Spanish, while during the next few minutes the interviewer asked students to speak in English. The conversations were taped and all three judges made determinations regarding subjects' language dominance based on these speech samples.

The conversations were recorded and the interviewer and two additional judges with expertise in bilingual education made assessments of each participant's language dominance. The criteria for selection of the three participating judges were a minimum of three years' experience in bilingual classrooms, a master's degree in bilingual education or a related area, and coursework or training in the field of language assessment. The judges' decisions regarding the subjects' language dominance were based on an individual student's overall ability to express himself or herself clearly in English and in Spanish. This assessment was based on the student's use of grammar, vocabulary, syntax, fluency, and oral language comprehension.

Since no absolutely accurate method of determining language dominance has been established, it was believed that the use of bilingual judges would provide a basis on which validity of subjects' language as assessed by instruments could be compared. The use of two judges' combined opinions on language dominance demonstrated high percentages of agreement. However, the criterion for the actual language dominance of subjects' language dominance was agreement by all three judges. It was against this

Table 1
Comparison of Total Judges' Combined Opinions
and Total Instruments for Assessing Language Dominance

	N^c	Percent of Agreement	Lambda	Cramer's V	Significance
Inter-American					
Test	73	16%	+.26	+.39	.00
Crane	73	22%	+.26	+.43	.00
Crane					
Questionnaire	68	54%	+.48	+.57	.00
Language					
Dominance					
Questionnaire	63	66%	+.48	+.53	.00

^{c} The total numbers used for this analysis were dependent on judges' agreement of language dominance as well as agreement with categories as determined by the selected instrument.

measure that each instrument was then compared and analysis of agreements and relationships were completed.

In addition, all participating students were administered the three instruments identified above. The tests were administered by trained testers who were bilingual in Spanish and English. Tests were administered within one month after the interview had been taped. This was done in an attempt to control for the effects of increased language skills through specific language classes provided in the participating schools. It was a method to determine that students' language skills would be relatively similar at the time the independent variables were administered.

Each student completed the Inter-American Test of General Abilities (Oral Vocabulary subtest). The student first completed this paper and pencil test in Spanish and then its alternate form in English. On a subsequent day the Crane Oral Dominance Test was administered to the student along with the accompanying optional questionnaire. Finally, the Pupil Questionnaire for Language Dominance Survey was completed by interviewing each student. The data were then analyzed to determine the relationship between the three measures of assessing language dominance and the bilingual judges' opinions.

FINDINGS

To ensure consistency in the opinions of the bilingual judges, inter-rater reliability was determined on their assessments of individual students. This process was completed through the use of cross-tabulation procedures. Overall, the judges were in agreement on the language dominance of students in 58 percent of the subjects reviewed. Of the twenty-eight students upon whose dominance all judges concurred, 6 percent were categorized as English dominant, 8 percent were categorized as Spanish dominant, and 44 percent were categorized as bilingual. All three judges were in agreement with respect to students' language dominance over half of the time. It would appear, then, that the unanimous opinions of the judges were consistent in terms of identifying specific language categories for these students.

The investigation studied four questions related to the problem of assessing students' language dominance. Each research question is stated below and findings specific to each are provided. Table 1 describes the comparisons between judges' opinions and the instruments for assessing language dominance.

1. What is the relationship between group-administered tests of language dominance and bilingual judges' opinions? Data analysis demonstrated that little relationship (16 percent agreement) existed between the Inter-American Test of General Abilities (Oral Vocabulary subtest), a group-administered test of language dominance, and the opinions of bilingual judges regarding students' language dominance. These results were not statistically significant.

2. What is the relationship between individually administered tests of language dominance and bilingual judges' opinions? A review of the data found that little relationship (22 percent agreement) existed between the opinions of bilingual judges and the Crane Oral Dominance Test. These results were not significant. However, while little agreement existed with bilingual judges, this instrument did reflect a slightly higher relationship with the judges than did the Inter-American Test of General Abilities.

3. What is the relationship between language surveys used to determine language dominance and bilingual judges' opinions? Two sociolinguistic questionnaires were included in this section. The first, the Pupil Questionnaire for Language Dominance Survey, proved to have the highest correlation (66 percent agreement) with bilingual judges' opinions, although these results were not found to be statistically significant. The second questionnaire, the optional portion of the Crane Oral Dominance Test, also demonstrated a substantially higher relationship (54 percent agreement) to judges' opinions when compared to other instruments included in the study. However, these results were not statistically significant.

4. What is the relative efficacy of group and individual language dominance tests, and language dominance survey forms in predicting language dominance as classified by bilingual judges? Each of the instruments included in this study was compared to determine the relationship different combinations of instruments had on the ability to predict language dominance from one another. The results of these combinations are discussed below. Table 2 provides information regarding inter-test comparisons.

The Inter-American Test of General Abilities (Oral Vocabulary subtest) was compared with the Crane Oral Dominance Test to determine the ability of one test to predict language dominance as determined by the second test. This combination proved to have a 46 percent rate of agreement (+0.15). However, the findings were not statistically significant, and it did demonstrate the lowest strength of association.

When the Inter-American Test of General Abilities (Oral Vocabulary subtest) was compared with both the Crane Questionnaire and the Pupil Questionnaire for Language Dominance Survey, results indicated little relationship existed (23 percent and 26 percent agreement respectively). Both of these sociolinguistic questionnaires had no predictive association with the Inter-American Test of General Abilities (Oral Vocabulary subtest).

When comparing the Crane Oral Dominance Test with the Crane Questionnaire and Pupil Questionnaire for Language Dominance Survey, little rate of agreement (27 percent and 21 percent agreement respectively) was evident. Once again, no predictive association was found. These results were not statistically significant.

Table 2
Inter-test Comparisons

Instruments Compared	Percent	Lambda	Cramer's V	Significance
Inter-American Test and Crane Oral Dominance Test	46%	.00	+.15	.20
Inter-American Test and Crane Questionnaire	23%	.00	+.20	.06
Inter-American Test and Pupil Questionnaire for Language Dominance Survey	26%	.00	+.21	.05
Crane Oral Dominance Test and Crane Questionnaire	27%	.00	+.29	.00
Crane Oral Dominance Test and Pupil Questionnaire for Language Dominance Survey	21%	.00	+.26	.00
Crane Questionnaire and Pupil Questionnaire for Language Dominance Survey	55%	.36	+.59	.00

Finally, when the Crane Questionnaire and the Pupil Questionnaire for Language Dominance Survey were compared they demonstrated the highest percentage of agreement of all comparisons of instruments included in the study (55 percent agreement). Further, their predictive association (+0.36) as well as their strength of association (+0.59) correlations were still relatively low and no statistical significance was found.

IMPLICATIONS

Administrators of bilingual programs may find it important to incorporate the following findings into their policy for the placement of bilingual students:

1. The findings indicate that group tests of language dominance reveal as much information as individual tests of language dominance. Since many programs of bilingual education are funded externally and are required to submit language dominance test data, what are the implications of the results of this study? Since no test measures all factors related to language dominance and since no one factor is more indicative of dominance than another at this point, then perhaps it is more reasonable to identify the most efficient and economical instrument for use in public school systems. In this case, then, a paper and pencil test which can be machine scored and administered to a group apparently will provide as much information as an individually administered test which a trained tester must administer, analyze, and score.

2. The results of this investigation demonstrated that sociolinguistic questionnaires generally substantiated opinions of bilingual judges regarding students' language dominance. Since these questionnaires are generally concise, it may be feasible to administer them to each child along with a group-administered test of language dominance in order to obtain a more precise picture of a child's language dominance. This additional information would then present a distinct perspective on the student's language use.

3. Perhaps an alternative method of assessing a student's language dominance is simply for trained bilingual judges to talk to the child. It may well be in a school district's best interest to utilize trained bilingual raters to assess the language dominance of its students. This alternative has several benefits. It may be economically sound in the long run for a school district to provide funds to train their teachers, who will then be able to provide these services for the school system over a period of years at minimal costs. By having direct contact with students, raters may be able to incorporate sociolinguistic information that could not be gleaned from simple paper and pencil tests.

4. A fourth and least desirable alternative for school systems is to continue to administer any test instrument for assessment of language dominance.

CONCLUSIONS

This study researched the problems inherent in the identification of reliable, efficient means of determining the language dominance of Hispanic students. Such research was required to examine the relationships between the tests of language dominance most widely used in Connecticut and the opinions of bilingual judges.

Results of the study indicate that little correlation exists between these selected tests and the judgments of bilingual interviewers. Further, the results suggest that there is little relationship among the tests themselves. While it is evident that more research in dominance testing is crucial, clearly the inconsistency in the results of current measures of language dominance reveal that conclusions based on such measures may well be unreliable. With increasing populations of nonnative English speakers in the public schools, it is essential that valid and reliable measures of determining linguistic facility be developed.

REFERENCES

Bordie, John G. "Language Tests and Linguistically Different Learners: The Sad State of the Art." *Elementary English* 47 (Oct. 1976): 814-28.

Cohen, Andrew D. "Bilingual Schooling and Spanish Language Maintenance: An Experimental Analysis." *Bilingual Review* 2, nos. 1-2 (Jan.-Aug. 1975): 3-12.

Cooper, Robert L. "Two Contextualized Measures of Degree of Bilingualism." *Modern Language Journal* 53, no. 3 (March 1969): 172-78.

Downie, N.M., and Heath, R.W. *Basic Statistical Methods.* 4th ed. New York: Harper and Row, 1974.

Dubois, Betty Lou. "Cultural and Social Factors in the Assessment of Language Capabilities." *Elementary English* 51 (Feb. 1974): 257-61.

Genesee, F.; Tucker, G.R.; and Lambert, W.E. "Communication Skills of Bilingual Children." *Child Development* 46 (Dec. 1975): 1010-14.

Mackey, William F. *Bilingual Education in a Binational School: A Study of Equal Language Maintenance through Free Alteration.* Rowley, Mass.: Newbury House, 1972.

Macnamara, John. "The Bilingual's Linguistic Performance—A Psychological Overview." *Journal of Social Issues* 2 (1967): 58-77.

Maurice, Louis J., and Roy, Robert R. "A Measurement of Bilinguality Achieved in Immersion Programs." *Canadian Modern Language Review* 32, no. 5 (May 1976): 575-81.

Melear, John D. "An Informal Language Inventory." *Elementary English* 51 (April 1974): 508-511.

Oller, John W. "Review Essay: The Measurement of Bilingualism." *Modern Language Journal* 60, no. 7 (1976): 399-400.

Paulston, Christina Bratt. "Linguistic and Communicative Competence." *TESOL Quarterly* 8, no. 4 (Dec. 1974): 347-62.

Politzer, Robert L. "Developmental Sentence Scoring as a Method of Measuring Second Language Acquisition." *Modern Language Journal* 58, nos. 5-6 (Sept.-Oct. 1974): 245-50.

Popham, W. James, and Sirotnick, Kenneth A. *Educational Statistics: Use and Interpretation.* 2d ed. New York: Harper and Row, 1973.

Silverman, Robert J., and Russell, Randall H. "The Relationships among Three Measures of Bilingualism and Their Relationship to Achievement Test Scores." Paper presented at AERA 1977 Annual Meeting, April 1977, New York City.

Spilka, Irene V. "Assessment of Second Language Performance in Immersion Programs." *Canadian Modern Language Review* 32, no. 5 (May 1976): 543-61.

Spolsky, Bernard, ed. *The Language Education of Minority Children: Selected Readings.* Rowley, Mass.: Newbury House Publishers, 1972.

Zirkel, Perry A. "The Why's and Ways of Testing Bilinguality Before Teaching Bilingually." *Elementary School Journal* 76, no. 6 (March 1976): 323-30.

_____ . "A Method for Determining and Depicting Language Dominance." *TESOL Quarterly* 8, no. 1 (March 1974): 7-16.

Bilingual Education: A Three-Year Investigation Comparing the Effects of Maintenance and Transitional Approaches on English Language Acquisition and Academic Achievement on Young Bilingual Children

Anthony R. Sancho

Semifinalist, Outstanding Dissertations
National Advisory Council on Bilingual Education

Degree conferred May 1980
The Claremont Colleges Graduate School
Claremont, California

Dissertation Committee:
Malcolm P. Douglass, *Chair*
Philip H. Dreyer
David E. Drew

About the Author

Dr. Anthony R. Sancho is president of the Minority Affairs Institute in Diamond Bar, California. He is also vice president of CHESS and Associates, and was an instructor at the University of California at Irvine. He has written on various aspects of bilingual education, including parent and community involvement and evaluation.

SUMMARY

The purpose of this study was to determine which of the two fundamental approaches to bilingual instruction, maintenance or transitional, would result in greater English language acquisition and academic achievement by young bilingual children through comparing their progress over a three-year period.

The two groups of students involved in the study were participating in a Title VII English-Spanish bilingual program in the Harlandale Independent School District in San Antonio, Texas. The research compared each group's accomplishments from 1976-77, their kindergarten year, through 1978-79, their second-grade year. Eight classrooms, four employing the maintenance model and four the transitional, were paired because of their similarity in terms of neighborhood setting, ethnic population, median family income, and median family school years completed.

The study examined entry-level language proficiency in both languages and three skill areas: English language, English reading, and mathematics. The acquisition of skills was measured by a norm-referenced instrument (CTBS) given yearly to the 110 students (53 in the maintenance model and 57 in the transitional) who were continuously enrolled in the project for the entire three years of the study.

The research employed a quasi-experimental design using a modified version of the time-series experiment as the basis for analyzing the data. Statistical techniques included two tailed t-tests, analyses of variance, and analyses of covariance.

Among the most significant findings were that the degree of proficiency that bilingual children bring to school in both languages has a direct relationship to their academic performance; the development and maintenance of two languages in the classroom increases the ability of bilingual children to perform logical and abstract operations such as those required in math; and the effects of either a maintenance or a transitional treatment are not as significant on achievement as the degree of linguistic competence that bilingual children initially bring to the school setting.

STATEMENT OF THE PROBLEM

Bilingual education, by definition, is controversial because it appears to strike at a foundation of U.S. schooling—English as the language of instruction. Bilingual schooling, even though practiced in the United States since the 1800s, is contrary to the established national norm of English-only instruction, a policy that was institutionalized around the turn of the century to consolidate the nation's territorial gains and solidify its political processes in light of the large numbers of immigrants entering the country (Leibowitz, 1971).

Even though the established English-only policy prevailed until the 1960s, it was a known fact that minority language children had difficulty in

English monolingual schools. The causes were considered to include lack of English language knowledge, low socioeconomic status, and inaccurate measuring instruments (Manuel, 1974).

In the 1960s there was growing recognition that minority language children needed some manner of special assistance if they were to have an equal opportunity to succeed in school. Initial efforts to overcome the problem took the form of supplemental English language development and what is commonly known as the English as a second language (ESL) approach, which attempted to intensify the acquisition of English language skills. This remedy did not satisfy minority language community leaders nor did it produce significant results.

As bilingual programs evolved and expanded under Title VII of the Elementary and Secondary Education Act, state legislatures also began passing legislation that built on the initiative of Congress. Quantitatively, bilingual education was beginning to meet the needs of linguistic minorities. The quality of this momentum, however, began to be questioned by many. Critics viewed the philosophy being employed as a remedial or compensatory approach to minority group education; they claimed that the use of the children's native languages in the school was perceived as an unfortunate necessity rather than an opportunity for enrichment. Thus, the ultimate aim was to move children out of functional bilingualism and into monoglot instruction as soon as possible (González, 1975). This approach, in essence, has come to be known as transitional bilingual education.

Many advocates of bilingual instruction foster a pluralistic approach that recognizes the minority and the English languages as vehicles for developing and maintaining skills in both languages, as well as a curriculum that integrates the customs and cultural history of the native language groups. This, in summary, is the maintenance approach.

The controversy between maintenance and transitional bilingual instruction, which is often referenced as a majority versus minority issue, has existed on a national basis since the inception of the 1968 Bilingual Education Act. The question is evident throughout the existing literature and it is inevitably raised at political and professional conferences, public hearings, and other gatherings related to bilingual education. Yet, in reviewing the literature and the available research, there is little evidence of any comprehensive effort to evaluate or compare the effects of either instructional approach on young children's acquisition of English and general academic achievement. The available writings address the issue from a philosophical or political base with minimal documentation of the effects on student accomplishment. This is not only evident as a result of this researcher's effort to identify available data, but it is also stated in the 1977 report of the National Advisory Council on Bilingual Education (NACBE). Quoting from the report, "research assessing and evaluating either model continues to remain inconclusive" (NACBE, 1977). Therefore, this study attempted to determine and compare the effects of both approaches on young bilingual children during their first three years in school, one of the most critical periods in a student's educational career.

PURPOSE OF THE STUDY

Considering the dearth of available research data and the continuous debates as to the merits of bilingual education, this study was undertaken to determine which of the two fundamental approaches to bilingual instruction, maintenance or transitional, would result in greater academic achievement by bilingual children.

The investigation was based on the premise that bilingual education has been implemented in the United States for the purpose of increasing educational opportunities for linguistically different children and providing them an alternative that would allow them to function more fully in the U.S. educational process. As such, the study was restricted to a longitudinal, three-year comparison of the effects of the two above-mentioned approaches on student achievement in the areas of language, reading, and math, as measured by an English standardized achievement test extensively used throughout the United States, the *Comprehensive Tests of Basic Skills* (CTBS).

The basis of this study was a three-year evaluation of the Title VII Bilingual Program of the Harlandale Independent School District in San Antonio, Texas. Because of the unique experimental controls applied to the programmatic features of the project, it was ideal for pursuing this investigation, which incorporated evaluation findings into a research context that will add to the information on bilingual education.

Evaluation differs from research, not in its methods, but in the purpose for which it is done. Evaluating educational programs calls for the application of research methods to an action context. That is, the investigation deals with people and programs in a real-life action environment. Evaluation is intended for use, whereas basic research puts the emphasis on the production of knowledge and leaves its use to the natural process of dissemination.

STATEMENT OF HYPOTHESIS

In examining which of the two approaches to bilingual instruction produces greater achievement in basic skills among bilingual children, the hypothesis for this study is that **there will be no statistically significant difference between the scores of students taught through either approach when these skills are measured by an English norm-referenced test.** For the purpose of this study, *basic skills* refers to the areas of language, reading, and math.

STATEMENT OF LIMITATIONS

Due to the magnitude and complexity of issues surrounding the above hypothesis, it was necessary to limit the scope of the research in order to avoid the many criticisms associated with previous investigations of bilingual education. As such, this study attempted to control only for socioeconomic status of experimental sites, entry-level language proficiency of participating students, and educational treatment. Additionally, student achievement over the three-year period was limited to yearly measurement by an English standardized instrument. Student performance was compared using scaled scores between youngsters continuously enrolled in a transitional model and those participating in a maintenance situation during their kindergarten (1976–77), first-grade (1977–78), and second-grade (1978–79) years. A comparison was also made between those students who remained in the program and those who dropped out after the first and second years. All children involved in the study possessed some degree of bilingualism.

Due to the legal mandate imposed by the *Lau* v. *Nichols* decision, children identified as non- or limited-English speaking must receive some form of special instruction to overcome this language deficiency. Thus, it was impossible to establish a control group for comparison purposes of non- and limited-English-speaking students who are not participating in English as a second language (ESL) or bilingual classes.

RESEARCH QUESTIONS

Based on the controls and the study design, this investigation attempted to answer the following questions:

1. Which of the two approaches to bilingual instruction provides bilingual children a better mode for academic achievement when compared via an English norm-referenced test?

2. To what extent does the linguistic competence that bilingual children initially bring to school affect their academic achievement in English?

3. To what extent does the socioeconomic environment of bilingual children affect their academic achievement in English?

4. Were there differences between the characteristics and achievement of the students who remained in the program for the full three years and those who dropped out after the first and second years?

The first question addresses the major issue of this study. The other three are directed at dimensions or variables that have traditionally influenced educational outcomes. For this reason the study design includes controls that provide answers to these questions.

TYPE OF EXPERIMENTAL DESIGN

The study followed a quasi-experimental design. As stated by Campbell and Stanley (1963), "There are many natural social settings in which the research person can introduce something like experimental design into his scheduling of data collection procedures (e.g., the *when* and *to whom* of measurement), even though he lacks the full control over the scheduling of experimental stimuli (the *when* and *to whom* of exposure and the ability to randomize exposures) which makes a true experiment possible. Collectively, such situations can be regarded as quasi-experimental designs."

The design was a modified version of the time-series experiment, the essence of which Campbell and Stanley (1963) describe as, "the presence of a periodic measurement process on some group and the introduction of an experimental change into this time series of measurements..." (p. 34).

For this study the time-series design was used on both groups of students, one receiving maintenance instruction and the other, transitional. A longitudinal (three-year) comparison was then made between the two groups using standard scores derived from CTBS-normed data. Statistical techniques applied to the data included two tailed t-tests, analyses of variance (ANOVA), and analyses of covariance (ANCOVA).

SAMPLING

The analyses of the data for the two student groups were conducted in a series of steps. Each step was taken so as to ultimately determine if major or significant differences existed between either approach. The first procedure was to examine the distribution of students in both tracks based on their initial language classification. Since all students in the study possessed some degree of bilingualism, entry-level language proficiency was used as a control. The students were assessed for language skills in the fall of the kindergarten year using the *Bilingual Syntax Measure* (BSM). An additional control used in the study was the socioeconomic status of each school as determined by the median family income of their respective census tracks. These controls were used as an attempt to establish matched groups upon which the ensuing data analyses would be done.

On the basis of BSM assessment, the students were classified into the following four language categories: special diagnosis, Spanish dominant, English dominant, or balanced bilingual. For the purpose of computer analyses these classifications were assigned numerical values of 0-1-2-3, respectively. These values align with the BSM coding system.

Overall, the distribution of students classified as less than English dominant and conversely English dominant or balanced bilingual was approximately the same for both instructional approaches. Forty-five percent of the students in the maintenance group were classified as special diagnosis or Spanish dominant (non-English proficient), while 49 percent of the students in the transitional model were categorized as such. A total of 54 percent of the maintenance and 50 percent of the transitional students were initially identified as English dominant or balanced bilingual (English proficient).

An examination of the distribution of students utilizing an x^2 analysis revealed that there was no statistically significant ($x^2 = 0.16$, df = 1) difference between the two approaches with respect to the number of students classified as non-English proficient and English proficient. Thus, it can be assumed that the sampling population was compatible.

SUMMARY OF FINDINGS

The major findings of the study revealed some interesting results that are worth reviewing. It is anticipated that these outcomes will have significant implications for future investigations related to bilingual education. The following summary highlights these major findings:

1. In comparing the overall achievement between the two groups using the two tailed t-tests, significant differences occurred only in math. These differences were in favor of the maintenance group. However, when the analyses of covariance were conducted to adjust for initial differences, the transitional students showed superior results in reading. The maintenance group again demonstrated significantly better results when this analysis was conducted for math.

   The transitional model emphasized the acquisition of English language skills and English reading. Thus, it stands to reason that by the end of the third year transitional students would do better in reading. On the other hand, the maintenance approach emphasized equal acquisition of skills in both languages. In a subject area like math, this group was able to acquire computational skills through the vehicle of both languages, thus facilitating the development of these skills regardless of their initial language proficiency.

2. In addition to analyzing the overall impact of the educational treatment on the two groups, analyses were performed to examine differences in achievement on the basis of the four initial language classifications. When the analysis of variance was done on each variable—reading, language, and math—the balanced bilingual group, regardless of instructional approach, performed significantly better in all three areas. It is interesting to note that they even surpassed the English dominant students. This result follows the assumption that students who have control of a first and a second language acquire a linguistic base superior to that of students who control only one language, even if it is their first one.

3. The analyses of variance that were used to examine the impact of socio-economic status (SES) on students' achievement revealed only one major finding. The students from the lowest SES achieved statistically greater scores in reading and math at the end of the first year. This result is perhaps attributed to the assumption that formal educational treatment has a greater initial effect on students who come from lower socioeconomic environments, since traditionally this setting does not encourage the development of cognitive skills prior to entering school.

4. In summarizing the characteristics of the students who dropped out of the program, very few significant differences occurred between the types of students leaving either approach. One significant finding is that more students classified as non-English proficient dropped out of the maintenance model than out of the transitional. It is possible that this was caused by parental decisions to remove their children from a program that was not maximizing their acquisition of English. On the other hand, more English-proficient students dropped out of the transitional approach than out of the maintenance. This occurrence might be due to the fact that in the first two years more instructional time was devoted to Spanish. It is possible that parents of English-proficient students preferred that their children receive instruction in English.

It is also interesting to note that the drop-out students in the lowest socioeconomic category achieved greater scores in reading and math than drop-out students in the other two SES categories. This result is similar to the finding among the lowest SES students who remained in the program for all three years. That is, they too achieved greater scores in reading and math than students in the other two SES categories at the end of the first year.

CONCLUSIONS

The hypothesis of this study was that there would be no statistically significant difference between the scores of bilingual students taught through either a maintenance or a transitional bilingual approach when basic skills were measured by an English norm-referenced test. This null hypothesis was formulated on the assumption that the long-standing controversy surrounding the two instructional approaches was more political than academic; therefore, no real difference between student achievement could be directly attributed to either educational treatment. As can be seen by the statistical results, the hypothesis could not be proven as stated. Some significant differences did occur.

The findings verify the complex nature of the question and support the need for further investigations of the many factors that affect the bilingual child's performance in school. Thus, the debate of maintenance versus transitional bilingual instruction appears to be a gross oversimplification of the problem. Justification for this position is based on a review of the data and the responses to the research questions.

1. Which of the two approaches to bilingual instruction provides bilingual children a better mode for academic achievement when compared via an English norm-referenced test? In comparing the overall results of the two groups for the three-year period it is obvious that neither approach, per se, is more advantageous. In terms of overall reading, the t-test analysis found no significant differences between the groups. When ANCOVA was applied, the transitional students showed better results. The language scores showed no significant differences either in the t-test analysis or ANCOVA. Significant, however, are the findings in mathematics where most of the data indicate that the achievement of the maintenance group was superior.

These results support the premise that educational treatment for bilingual children should not be simplified to the level of offering only two alternative approaches.

The findings in reading for the transitional students are probably attributed to the goal of that instructional approach, which is to focus on the acquisition of English language and reading skills. The fact that they showed superior results because of their performance the last year of the study suggests that indeed that approach was starting to meet its objective. The lesser achievement of the maintenance group in English reading can probably be ascribed to the fact that much of their literacy development was done in Spanish.

The t-test and ANCOVA analyses both showed no overall significant difference between either group. These findings are likely the result of the emphasis given in both approaches to English language development. It is interesting to note, however, that transitional students gained English language skills at a faster rate than the maintenance children. This again is in keeping with the goal of the transitional approach.

The superior performance of the maintenance group in mathematics during the study supports other recent research findings that claim that mother tongue development is especially important in school subjects that require abstract modes of thought. Skutnabb-Kangas and Toukomaa in their study of Finnish immigrant students report that reaching the abstraction level of the mother tongue is important for mastering the conceptual operations connected with mathematics.

In reviewing the overall results related to this research question, it can be tentatively concluded that bilingual treatment should be revamped to accommodate a combination of instructional approaches that produce the desired results. For example, if a transitional mode is more appropriate for the development of English reading skills, then that treatment can be applied to that curriculum area. On the other hand, if a maintenance method is more beneficial in a subject such as mathematics, then the use and maintenance of two languages could be channeled to those curriculum tracts.

2. To what extent does the linguistic competence that bilingual children initially bring to school affect their academic achievement in English? In terms of overall achievement based on language classification, the students initially categorized as balanced bilinguals exceeded the three other language groups in all the assessed areas—language, reading, and mathematics—regardless of the instructional approach employed. This finding suggests that there is a direct relationship between the bilingual child's ability to control two languages and achievement in school. In other words, the greater the ability to manipulate two language systems, the greater the facility for positive acquisition of basic skills. This implies that the degree of linguistic competence that is developed in bilingual children prior to entering school is more crucial than the formal instructional approach provided in the school setting. The goals of either language maintenance or language shift did not seem to have as significant a bearing on the outcomes, since the balanced bilingual children were evenly distributed between the two instructional approaches.

3. To what extent does the socioeconomic environment of bilingual children affect their academic achievement in English? When socioeconomic status was used as a control, there were no consistent findings that allowed for definitive conclusions to be drawn. Perhaps the degree of differentiation between the three SES groups in this study was not great enough to see significant differences. It is important to note, however, that the youngster in the lowest SES group did achieve statistically significant higher scores in reading and math for the study's first year (1976–77). This can probably be attributed to what other researchers, such as Cummins (1979), claim to be a common occurrence among children of lower SES. That is, students from lower socioeconomic environments are more dependent on the school to provide the prerequisites for linguistic and cognitive development. However, because no major difference occurred among the three groups over the three-year period, one can summarize that in this study SES did not play a significant role in the students' academic achievement.

4. Were there any differences between the characteristics and achievement of students who remained in the program the full three years and those who dropped out after the first and second years? The findings related to this research question indicate that there was a minimal difference between the characteristics and achievement of the students who remained in the program and those who dropped out. Of those in the attrition group, more English-proficient students remained in the maintenance model than in the transitional. Conversely, more students classified as non-English proficient remained in the transitional model than in the maintenance. It is also interesting to note that most attrition occurred at the end of the first year. The conclusions that can be drawn from these findings are primarily based on assumptions made by this researcher, since available data did not address the causes of attrition. However, on the basis of discussions with the project's coordinator and the evaluator, there was considerable concern among parents of the students at the program's onset as to the effects that the two approaches would have on their children. Since most parents want their children to succeed in school, the necessity to acquire English language skills played a major function in their response to the program. It is perhaps this phenomenon that contributed to the results which showed that the maintenance approach retained more English-proficient students and the transitional, which has as its major goal the acquisition of English, maintained more of the non-English proficient students. Parents of non-English-proficient students tended to be more approving of the transitional program, while parents of English-proficient students were more secure in letting their children maintain their English while increasing their Spanish skills.

IMPLICATIONS

The results of this study should be viewed within the constraints of the variables and controls used. The major implications that can be drawn, however, are the following:

1. The limitations imposed by providing bilingual instruction through the vehicle of either a maintenance or transitional approach are too narrow in scope for bilingual children. Allowances for combinations or variations seem more appropriate for these students.

2. The effects of either a maintenance or transitional instructional approach are not as significant on student achievement as the degree of linguistic competence that bilingual children initially bring to the school setting.

3. The degree of proficiency that bilingual children bring to the school in both languages seems to have a direct relationship to their academic performance.

4. The results of this study support the hypothesis that the development and maintenance of two languages in the classroom increase the ability of bilingual children to perform logical and abstract operations such as those required in math.

The longitudinal aspect of this study was intended to curb some of the past criticisms about the shortcomings associated with studies examining the effects of bilingual education. The complex nature of language and its acquisition as well as the evolutionary features of cognitive development require that the impact of educational treatment coupled with student input be reviewed over time. The failure to do so has often led to rash misjudgments and consequently serious detriment to the participants in what is intended to be "equalized" educational opportunity.

The limitations imposed on this study were intentional, to narrow the investigation to basic skill areas. Additionally, the restriction of examining only results of English norm-referenced assessments was intended to see how the two instructional approaches affect bilingual children's performance in the areas that tend to cause most concern among U.S. public school personnel and parents.

Because this study is one of the initial attempts to examine the effects of maintenance versus transitional bilingual approaches over time, the results should be interpreted as such. Three years is a short time compared to the total span of an educational career. Therefore, this effort may be considered a beginning step toward the many investigations that should be conducted. It is concluded in this study that an attempt to examine the educational needs of bilingual children only in terms of these two instructional approaches is a gross oversimplification of the many factors that affect their total development. It is hoped that the findings presented in this study will stimulate other researchers to pursue future investigations of bilingual children's development in a U.S. public school setting.

REFERENCES

Campbell, D.T., and Stanley, J. *Experimental and Quasi-Experimental Designs for Research.* Chicago: Rand McNally and Co., 1963.

Cummins, James. "Linguistic Interdependence and the Educational Development of Bilingual Children." *Review of Educational Research* 49, no. 2 (1979): 222-251.

González, Josué. "Coming of Age in Bilingual/Bicultural Education: An Historical Perspective." In *Inequality in Education: Bilingual/Bicultural Education.* Cambridge: Harvard University Center for Law and Education, 1975.

Leibowitz, A.H. *Educational Policy and Political Acceptance: The Imposition of English as the Language of Instruction in American Schools.* Washington, D.C.: Center for Applied Linguistics, 1971.

Manuel, Herschel. "The Education of Mexican-American and Spanish-Speaking Children in Texas." Austin, Texas: University of Texas Fund for Research in the Social Sciences, 1930. Reprinted in *Education and the Mexican American.* New York: Arno Press, 1974.

National Advisory Council on Bilingual Education (NACBE). *Third Annual Report of the National Advisory Council on Bilingual Education.* Rosslyn, Va.: InterAmerica Research Associates, 1977.

Skutnabb-Kangas, T., and Toukomaa, P. *Teaching Migrant Children's Mother Tongue and Learning the Language of the Host Country in the Context of the Socio-Cultural Situation of the Migrant Family.* Helsinki: The Finnish National Commission for UNESCO, 1976.